# CELTIC DESIGN

**Aidan Meehan** studied Celtic art in Ireland and Scotland and has spent the last two decades playing a leading role in the renaissance of this authentic tradition. He has given workshops, demonstrations and lectures in Europe and the USA, and more recently the Pacific North West from his home base in Vancouver, B.C., Canada.

D1039843

# CELTIC DESIGN

# A BEGINNER'S MANUAL

AIDAN MEEHAN

With 258 illustrations

THAMES AND HUDSON

Also published in this series

KNOTWORK: THE SECRET METHOD OF THE SCRIBES

Any copy of this book issued by the publisher as a paperback is sold subject to the condition that it shall not by way of trade or otherwise be lent, resold, hired out or otherwise circulated without the publisher's prior consent in any form of binding or cover other than that in which it is published and without a similar condition including these words being imposed on a subsequent purchaser.

artwork and calligraphy
Copyright © 1991 Aidan Meehan

All Rights Reserved. No part of this publication may be reproduced or transmitted in any form or by any means, electronic or mechanical, including photocopy, recording or any other information storage and retrieval system, without prior permission in writing from the publisher.

Printed and bound in Great Britain

# CONTENTS


| | | |
|---|---|---|
| | Introduction | 6 |
| I | Step Patterns | 7 |
| II | Key Patterns | 23 |
| III | Early Celtic Spirals | 39 |
| IV | Geometry of the Spiral | 58 |
| V | Irish Half Uncial Script | 71 |
| VI | How to lay out a manuscript page | 87 |
| VII | How to decorate letters | 100 |
| | Conclusion | 144 |
| | Appendix: tools, materials, techniques | 145 |

# Introduction

HERE for the first time is a manual of Celtic design for beginners which gives the form of construction of step patterns and key patterns based on the hitherto secret grid method of the scribes. This method is simple, a matter of joining the dots.

Almost as simple is the freehand construction of the spiral, given here along with a selection of treatments from early Celtic metalwork.

Compass work is also important to Celtic design, and here it is combined with the construction of letters, the decoration of which is suggested as an application.

# STEP PATTERNS

Step patterns, found in the illuminated books, metal- and stonework, are very simple, and illustrate the intelligibility of form that characterises Celtic pattern. Here are a few examples for you to reproduce.

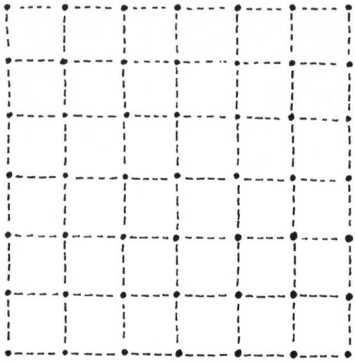

a. Six-square grid.

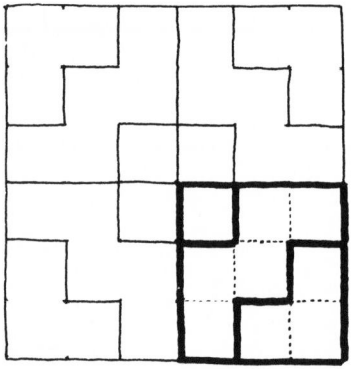

b. Same grid; each quarter is a three-square step pattern.

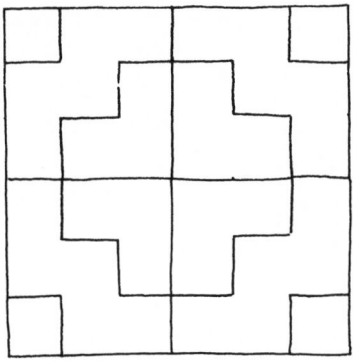

c. The quarters rearranged.

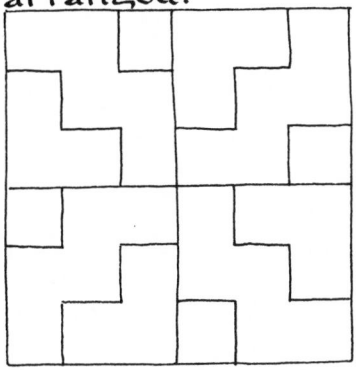

d. Same three-square unit in six-square grid.

Usually the design is worked out on a simple square grid of dots in which repeats of a smaller unit may be arranged in different combinations as here, a, b, c, d. These patterns, b, c, d, are based on the smaller repeat, b.

a. This one is made of four units, each one based on a four-square grid. Together the four units fill an eight-square.

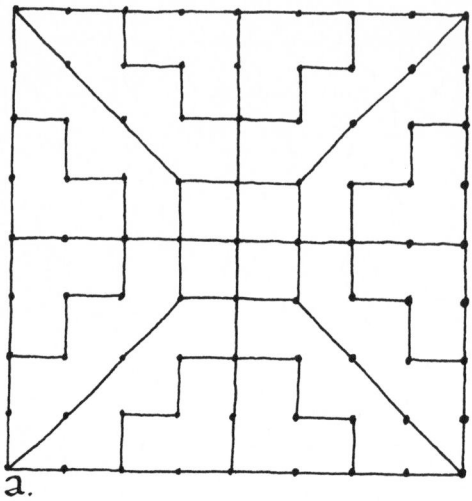
a.

b. If we change the order of the tiles, this is one result.

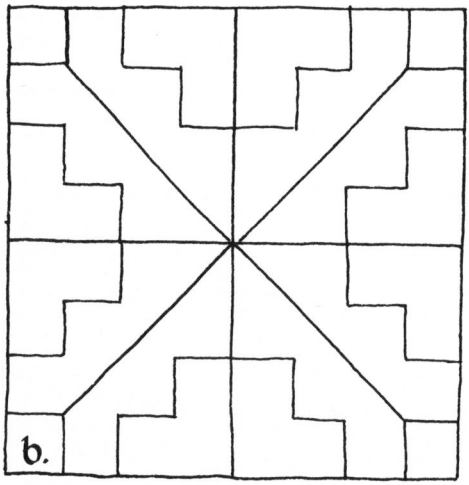
b.

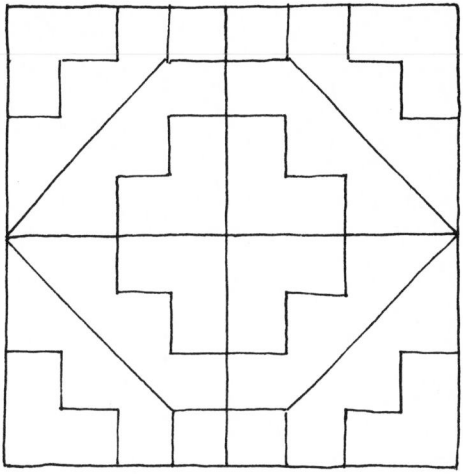

a.

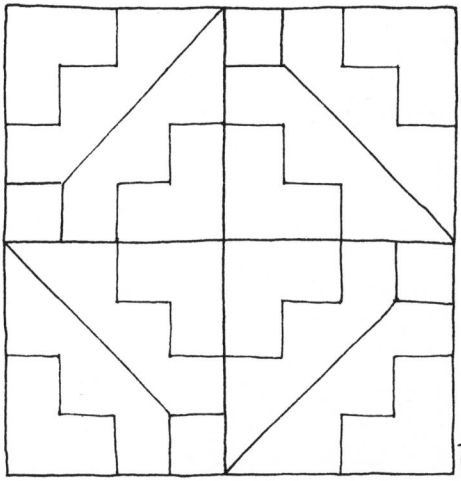

b.

On this page, the same eight-square grid has been used, and the quadrants are identical. Only their arrangement has been changed.

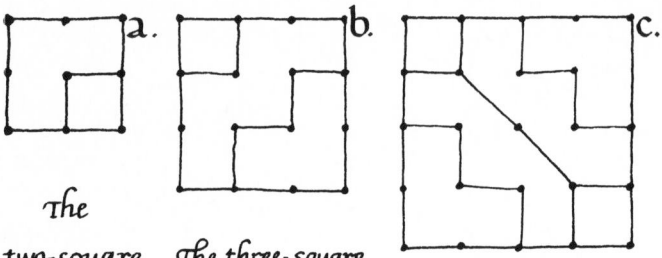


The two-square

The three-square

The four-square

A GREAT many beautiful overall patterns may be produced by the tile method, as shown on previous pages. The three-square, b, is used on pages 8 and 9. The four-square, c, is a variation of the tile unit used in the patterns on page 10 and 11.

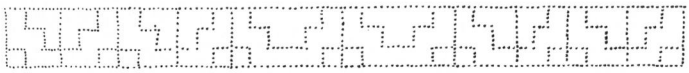

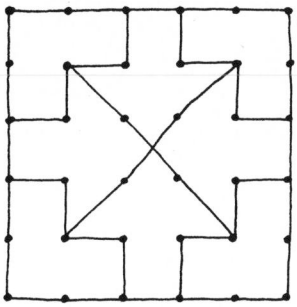

d.

The five-square

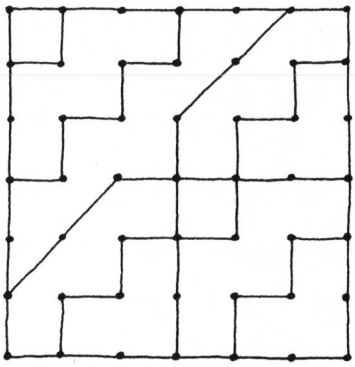

e.

The six-square

In these two we see the diagonal line used, as on previous page, c, to tie-in points on the grid otherwise floating free of the step lines. A single square might also have been used to connect the centre dots of fig. d.

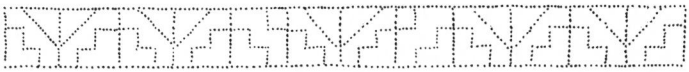

PATTERNS are pleasing when they are reasonably well balanced. The two-square tile, *a*, below, is not balanced, yet four units make a very balanced pattern, *b*, that fills a four-square grid.

Three tiles will fit a six-square along each side, *c*, but the result is not a pattern. It is useful as a tile, though, and could be

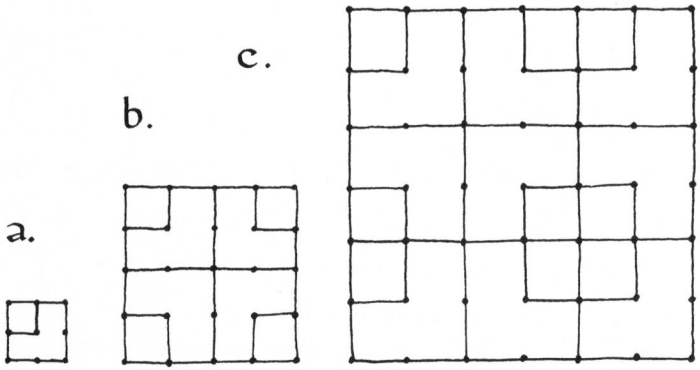

arranged in each quarter of a twelve-square dot grid.

The pattern below is on an eight-square grid, *d*. Each quarter is the same design as that on the opposite page, *b*, used here as a tile. In the middle of the pattern, *d*, a further tile unit emerges. Compare this unit, *e*, with that at *b*. The respective modules are shown at *f* and *a*.

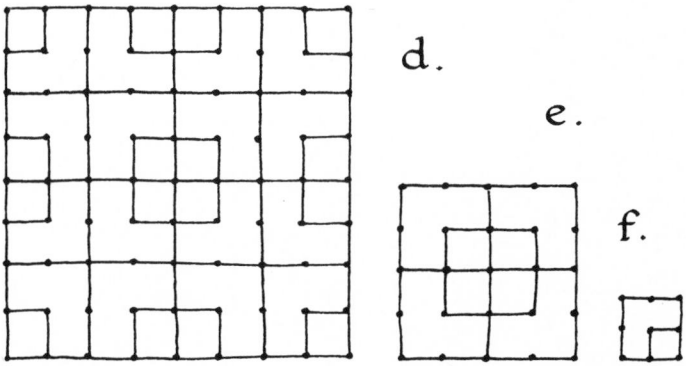

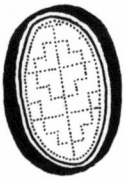

ON this page, the three-square tile, *a*, is expanded to fill a six-square and a twelve-square lay-out. Four units combine to form the six-square, *b*. In turn, four of these make up the larger square, *c*. The centre four tiles in *fig.c* provide a further variation.

On page 17, a four-square tile : compare with pages 10, 11.

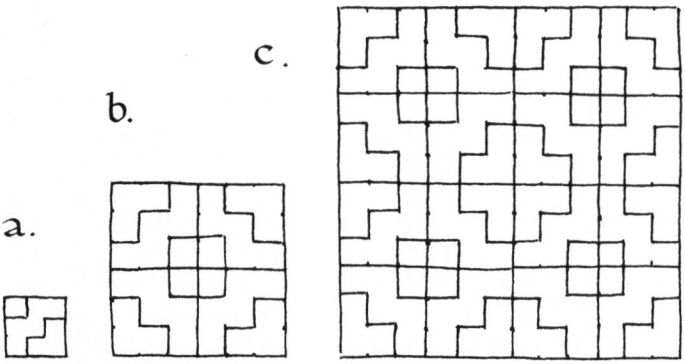

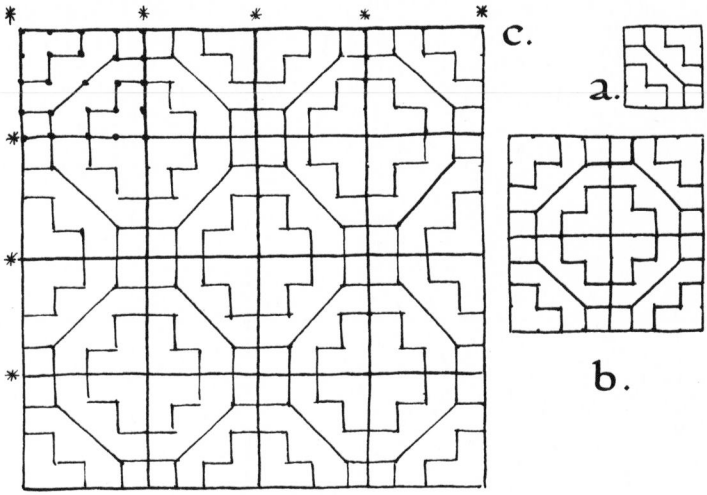


IN the manuscripts these step patterns are used as fillers, drawn freehand, or aided by a grid. To draw the grid for c, above, lay out the 4x4 squares in pencil, as indicated by asterisks. Then dot in the tile grid, as at top left, and ink in the lines, tile by tile.

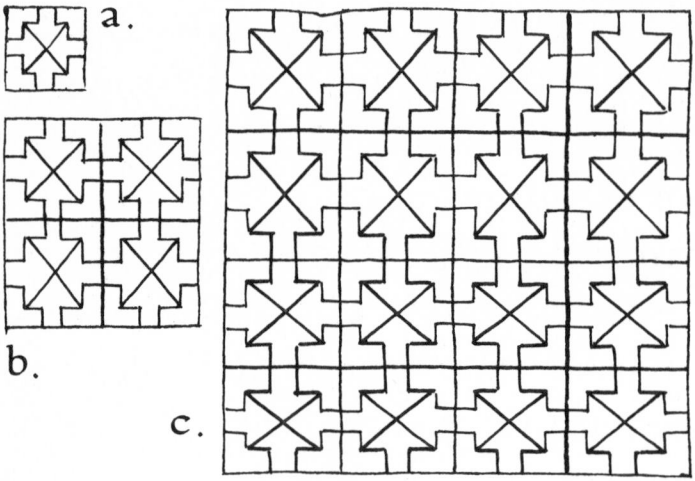


METALWORK is another art in which the Celtic artists used step pattern, this one from the Lemanahan shrine, Ireland, 12th century. The design above appears as an enamel stud. It joins all the dots of a five-by-five square grid. Repeated in four and sixteen units, b, c.

THIS beauty is showcased in the Book of Lindisfarne, in a major piece of work, one of the exceptions, for step patterns are usually neglected. But the type of design you see here represents a mature tradition in its bloom, a widely practised art form. It has been sadly overlooked, a fact that is

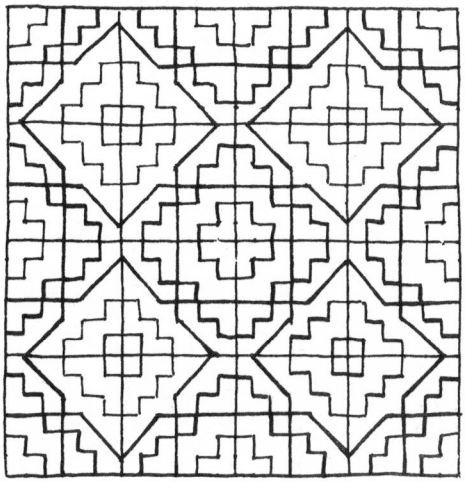

c.

a.

b.

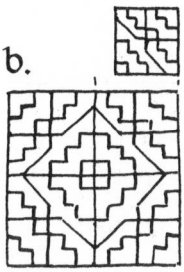

brought out by a search through the manuscripts.. there are few of any great, and a lot of very little interest. So the whole class is often overlooked, which is a pity. Master the step patterns. They provide a key to the metal smith's art of over-all grid layout: this is the basis of Celtic carpet-page design.

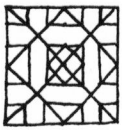

c.

a.

b.

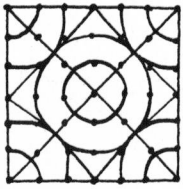

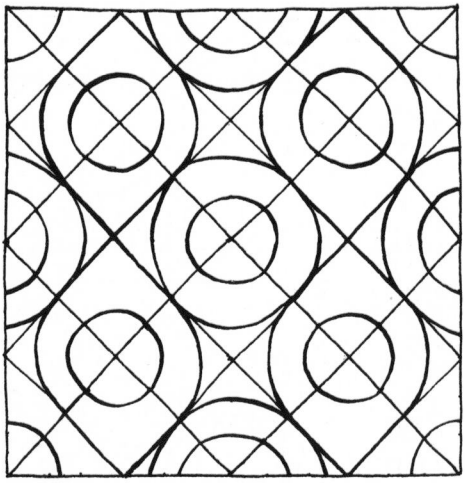

The pattern opposite, from the Book of Kells, uses circles instead of steps, but is developed from a grid, never the less, *a, c.*

Below, from the Book of Durrow, a combination of circle *and* step, derived from the six-square grid, *b.*

c.

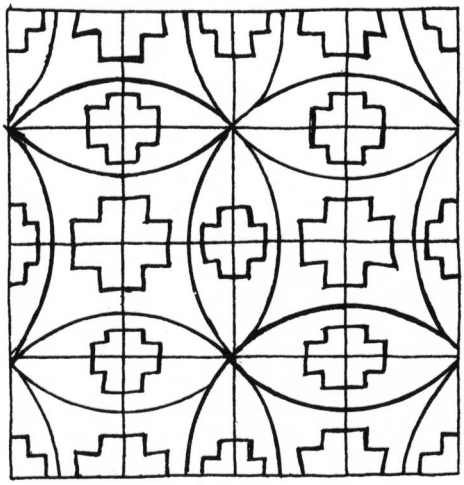

b.

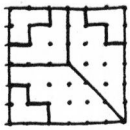

a.

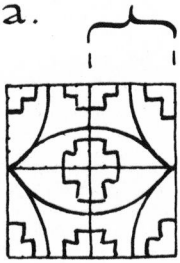

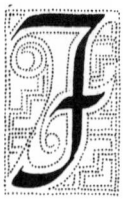

IG. b, on previous page has dots to spare that may be joined by step lines, a, then repeated, b, and outlined, c.

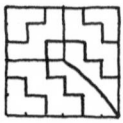

a.

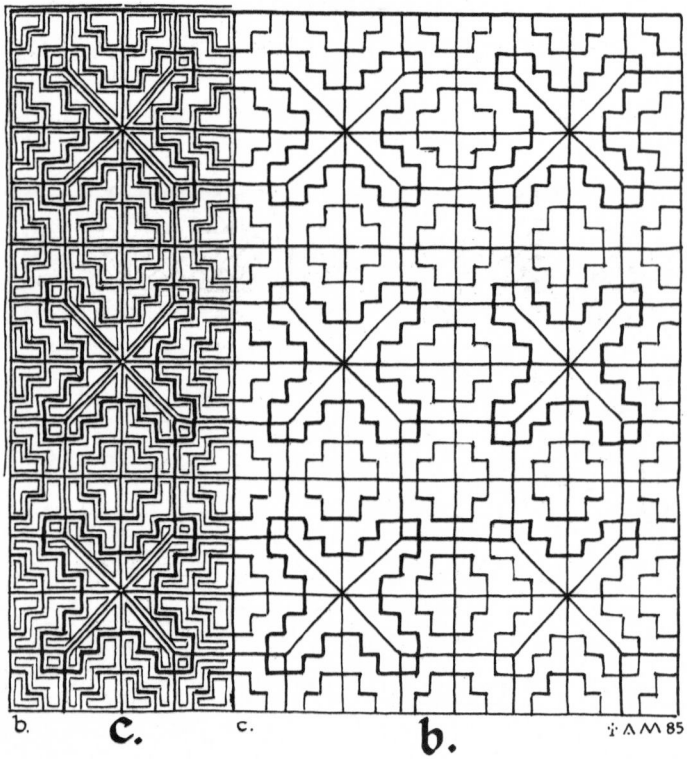

KEY PATTERNS go well with other kinds of Celtic pattern. Here, borders of step pattern and plait work combine with the cross of key pattern.

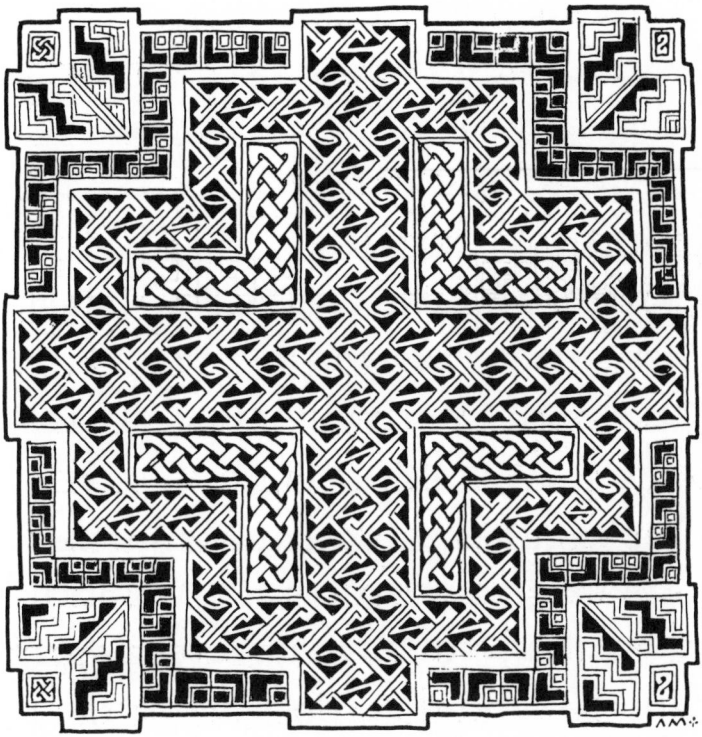

AS WITH STEP patterns and plaitwork, key patterns are easily made by join-the-dots. As in plaitwork, the lines are placed in such a way as to create paths.

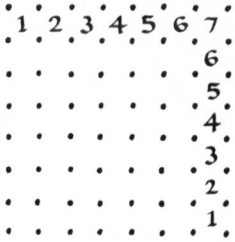


Fig. 1, a.

Fig. 1, b.

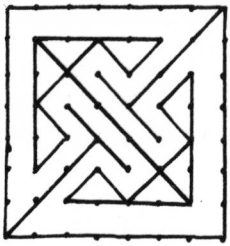

Key patterns are found worldwide. Celtic key patterns are based on a particular system, developed from a basic square building block, Fig. 1, b. The basic key pattern starts out on a square grid, 7 spaces across and 7 down, enclosed by the sides of a square. This box and these dots define the

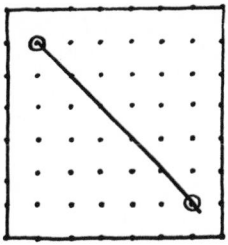

Fig. 2, a.

Fig. 2, b.

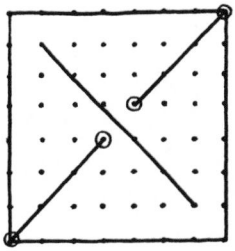

pattern.

In drawing the pattern, the lines follow a certain order. This is called the *stroke order*, as illustrated on this and the following pages, Fig. 2, a ~ j.

The diagonals should be drawn first, Fig. 2, a, b. The first diagonal goes through the middle cell, but not the corners, Fig. 2, a. The second cuts through the corners, not the centre. Fig. 2, b. Next draw the "arrow-heads" on the ends of the first diagonal, Fig. 2, c ~ f.

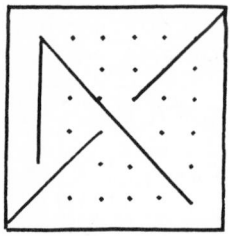

Fig. 2, c.

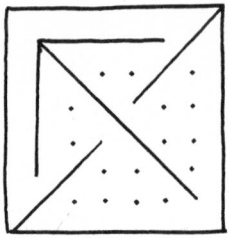

Fig. 2, d.

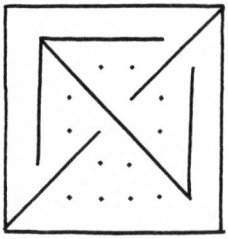

Fig. 2, e.

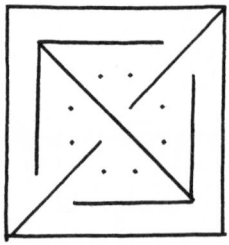

Fig. 2, f.

The arrow heads define the corners at each end of the diagonal stroke at fig. 2, a. This is why the corners must be avoided when drawing the first stroke, to accommodate the path.

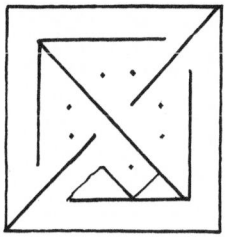

Fig.2g.

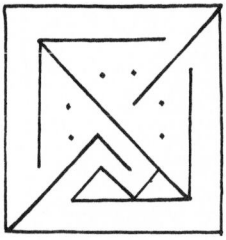

Fig.2,h.

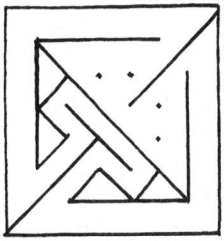

Fig.2,i.

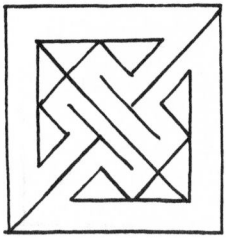

Fig.2,j.

On each arm of the arrowhead, draw a zig-zag, fig.2,g, which locks the "key", fig.2,h. Double the lock and key, fig.2,i. Repeat diagonally opposite, fig.2,j.

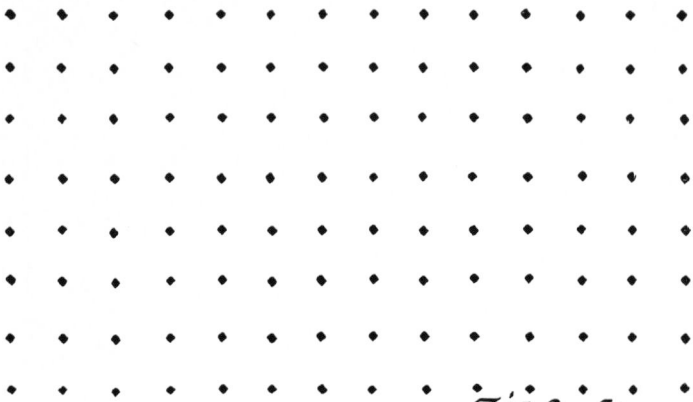

Fig. 3, a.

ON THE FOLLOWING PAGES, all the designs of *figs.* 3–6 are based on the grid above, which has thirteen spaces across, and seven down.

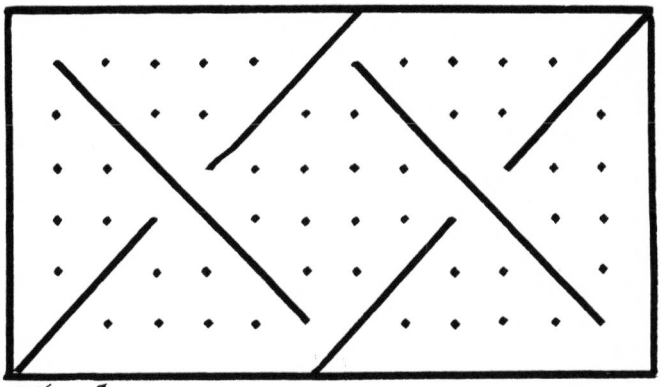

Fig 3,b.

On the grid lay the lines of the diagonals as before, first the unbroken stroke with a gap at each end, as in *fig. 2a*, then the broken diagonal, as in *fig. 2,b*. Complete the right-hand half of *fig. 3,b* only after having done the left side. Set off the whole diagonal first, directly below the intersection of the upper edge

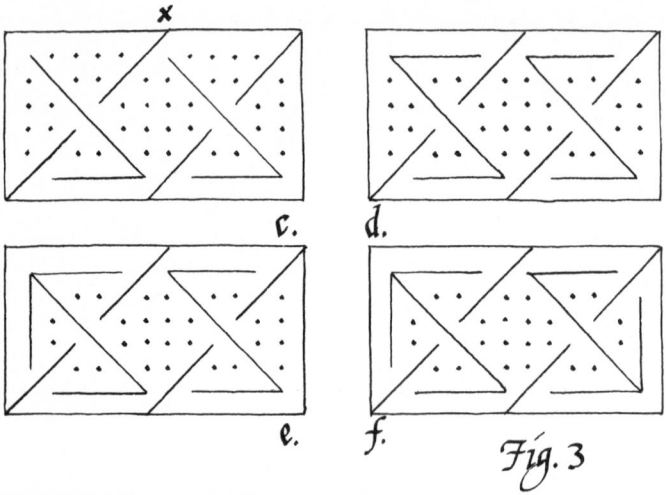


Fig. 3

with the broken diagonal already drawn, marked "x" above, f. 3, c. Check that the positions of the diagonals are exactly as in f. 3, b before proceeding. You can tell by the pattern of dots whether your lines are arranged correctly or not.

The next stage, the arrow-heads, includes two segments of path on

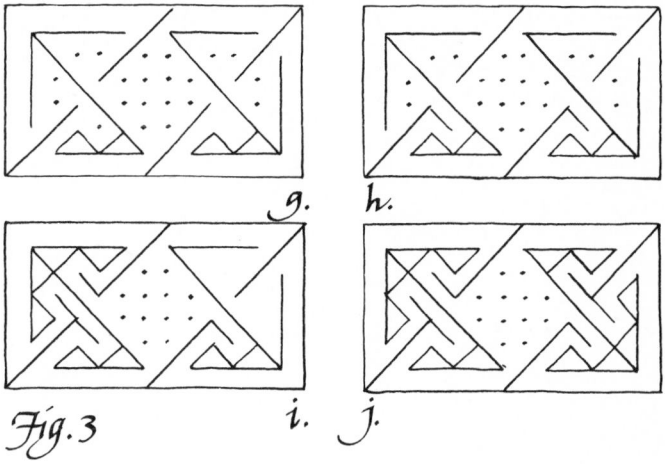


Fig. 3

the upper and lower edge of the rectangle, fig. 3, f. This completes the second stage. Check the dots to ensure lines are in order.

Third, complete the corners, fig. 3, j. The keys are all aligned along the edges. Only the centre diamond cell remains. Notice the form of the twelve dots in the diamond.

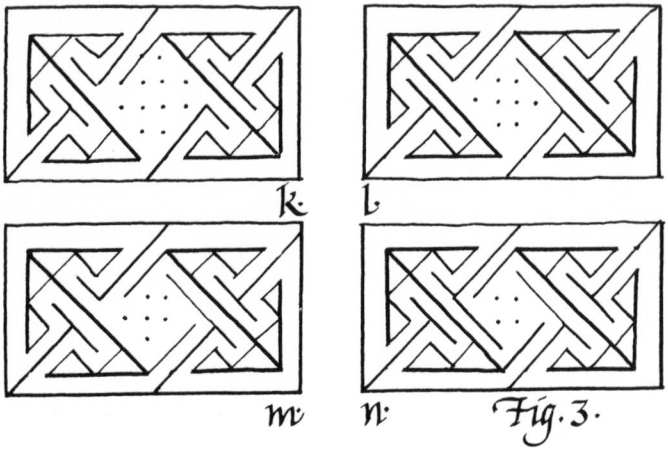


Fig. 3.

There are quite a few variants that can be made in the central cell, but first, the swastika key pattern. In the diamond of fig. 3, j, you will see four paths leading into the space. Extend these paths, fig. 3, k–r, to form the clockwise spiral in the middle, in two stages. The first stage is shown here, k–n.

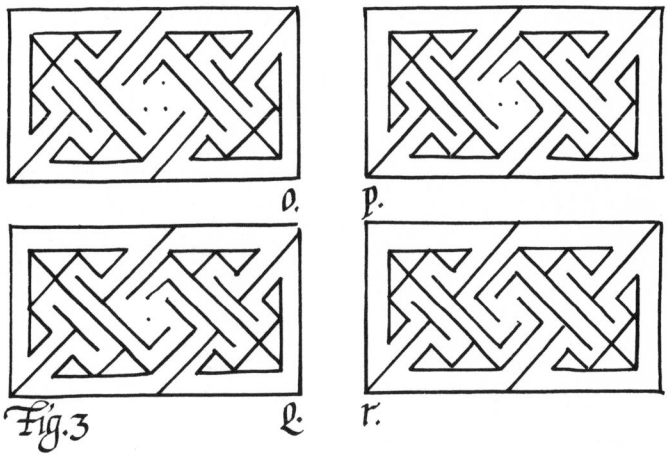


Fig.3

Make sure all four arms of the spiral in *fig.3,n*, are complete, and four dots remain. Now wind a final turn, as above, *fig. 3, o–r*.

The really significant part of this pattern is the layout of the diagonals and the keys around the edges and corners. Master steps *a–j, fig.3*, and the following variations will be easy.

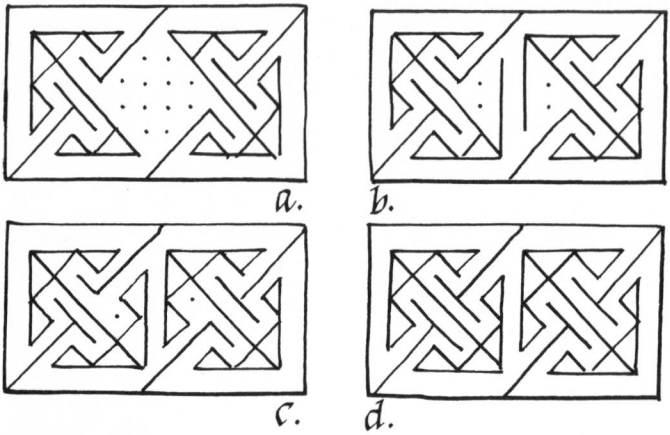


Fig.4.

DRAW the grid as in fig.3, and complete steps a~j up to the diamond with 12 dots, as above, fig.4,a.

Now complete the two arrow heads with a single path width between, as in fig.4,b.

Last, complete locks first, fig.4,c. either side of the vertical bar, fig.4,d.

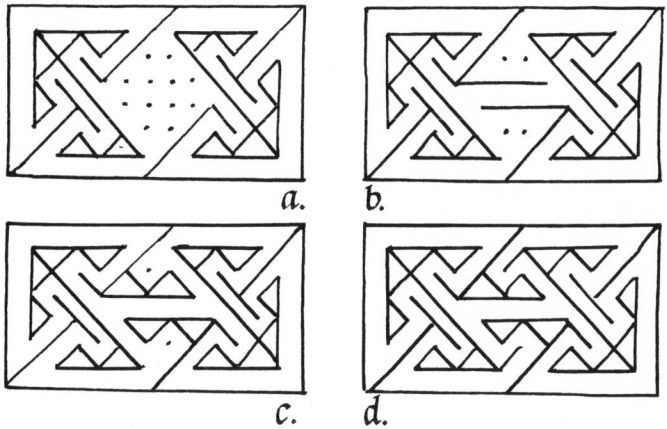


Fig. 5.

START This keypattern with the same build up as in the last one, but, instead of a vertical bar put in a horizontal, as in fig. 5,b, consisting of two parallel lines each springing from a key.

On the lines of the bar, put the zigzag lock, fig. 5c.

Complete key in each lock, fig. 5d.

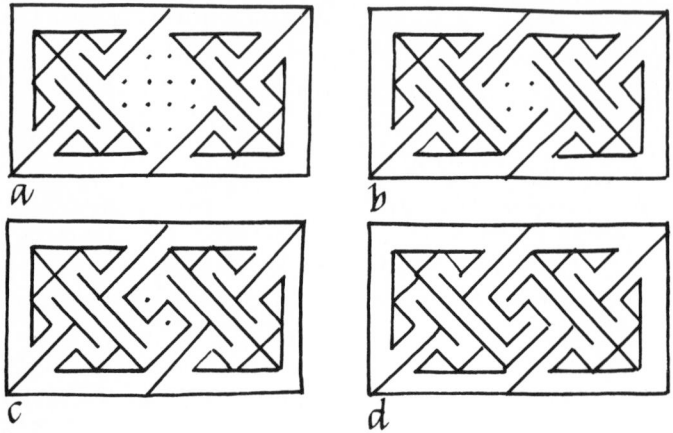


Fig. 6.

HERE the pattern follows fig. 3, a – n, to give the first turn of the clockwise spiral with four branches, fig. 6, b.

Two opposite branches may be connected by a zig zag stroke, fig. 6, c. These set off opposed locks.

Last, put keys in the locks, fig. 6, d.

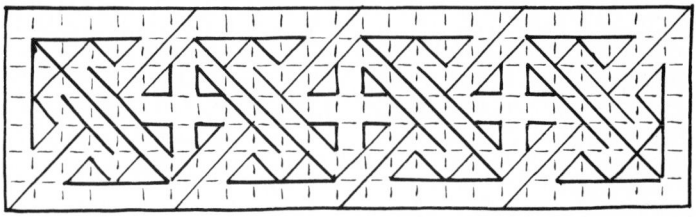

Fig. 7, a.

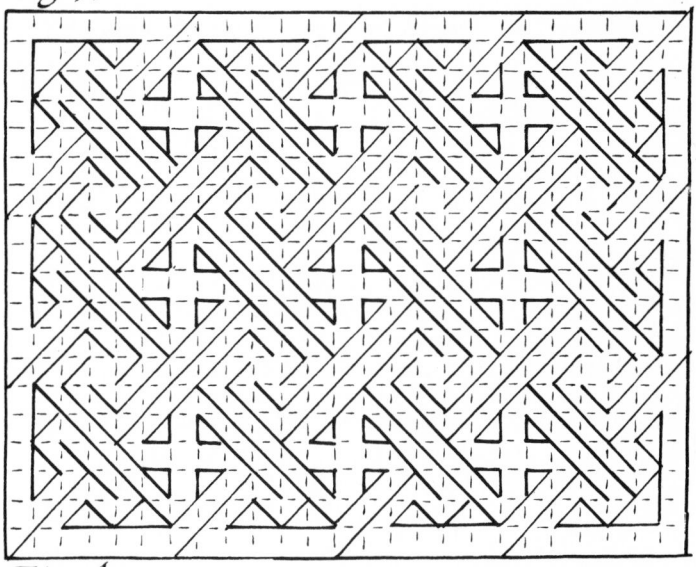

Fig. 7, b.

## Chapter 11

FIGURES 1 to 6 in this introductory outline show how the basic key pattern contains in its structure the seeds of all the mainstay variations used by the ancient scribes. There are of course other species sprung from different seed structures, but these more unusual key patterns can wait for now.

Fig. 7, a, introduces another diamond filler, in a repeat of four basic units on a square grid seven down and twenty-five across.

Fig. 7, b, is on a grid 25 x 19.

Leaving key patterns aside, for now, let us take a look at spirals with keys, let us play with spirals.

## SPIRALS: THE SINGLE SPIRAL.

Figure 1.

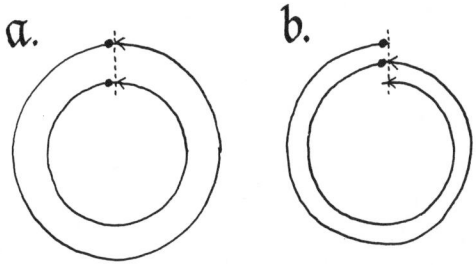


Compare the two figures above. The single spiral on the right turns twice, so it has the same effect as two concentric circles, *fig.* 1, a; that is, the inside is surrounded by a path separating it from the outside.

## Single Spiral: s~scroll.

Fig. 2

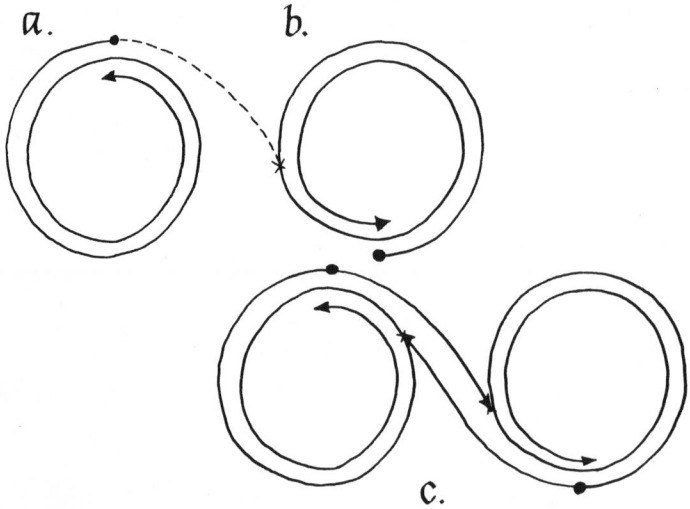


Two singles joined so the path leads from one to the other. Notice how the spiral at f.2,a, starts at the top, and f.2,b, starts at the bottom.

The path connecting the spirals is drawn with two lines. The first joins the outside of the path of the first spiral, f. 2,a, to the inside of the second, f. 2,b, as shown dotted here. The second line joins the bottom of b to the inside of the first spiral, f. 2,c. The path now leads from the inside of one spiral to the empty centre of the second. This integrates the design so that it may not be entered from without, being completely self-contained. In traversing the spiralling path you begin at the centre and end at the centre. We cannot expand further on this design externally, but we may elaborate the middle spaces.

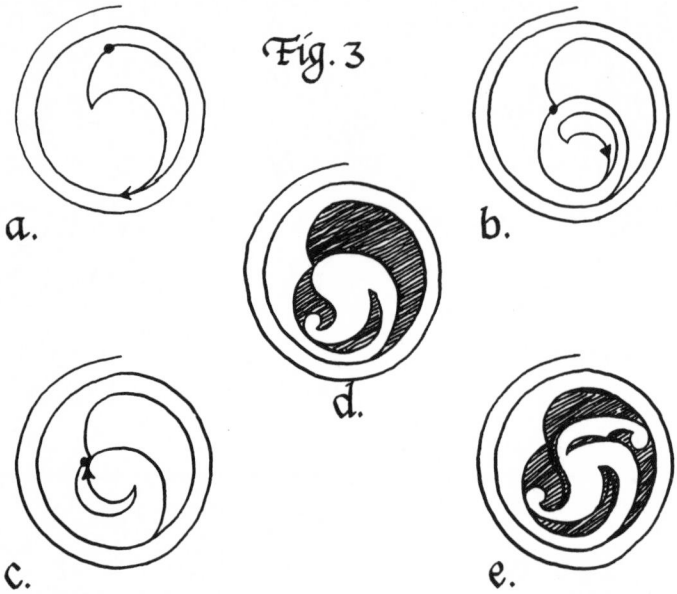


Fig. 3

Here you have five variations, all developed from the "comma" path ending, f. 3a, from which are derived f.s 3,b,c.

Figures 3,d and e are types of "duck-head" terminal. Figure 3,e is a "triskel".

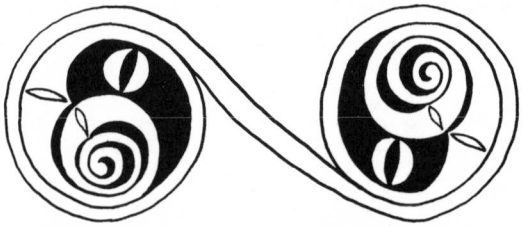

Fig. 4

The spirals on this s-scroll are identical, based on *fig. 3,b.* One is upside down in relation to the other. Any spiral in *fig. 3* may be treated as an s-scroll. A counter may be drawn to relieve the largest background space - such as the "eye" used here. This should not be overdone: one counter per largest background space is sufficient in most instances.

In *fig. 4* there is a second type of counter, to be used only where the path flares widest, called a "lens".

Fig. 5

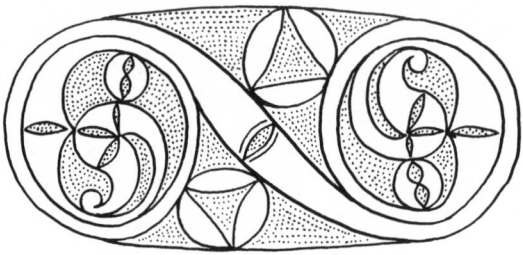

The spiral on the left is the same as at *fig. 3,d*, the "duck-head" terminal. Three lenses have been added in each duck-head, plus one at the widest point of the path. Inside the widest part of each spiral's background is a counter circle, containing two lenses. Between the two spirals the path diverges, at which point a bracketed lens, or "trumpet mouth", is used to counter the path's width.

The s-scroll may be enclosed with lines. The background is also countered.

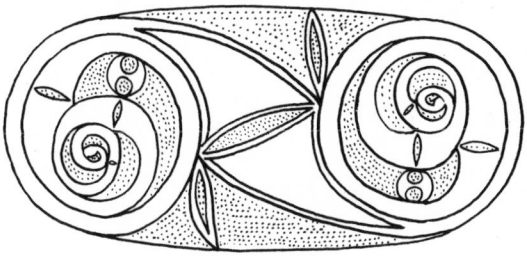

Fig. 6

In this figure, the path between the spirals has been made as wide as can be. With the path so wide as this, the centre lens may be outlined as shown, and the outline continued back along the path.

With so much path, the lenses either side of the cross over have been in-lined and filled-in, to counter as much as possible of the outer background.

Inside the spiral roundels the counter used - that looks like an apple-core - is called

SINGLE SPIRAL DUCK-HEAD TERMINAL *from* TORRS PONY CAP

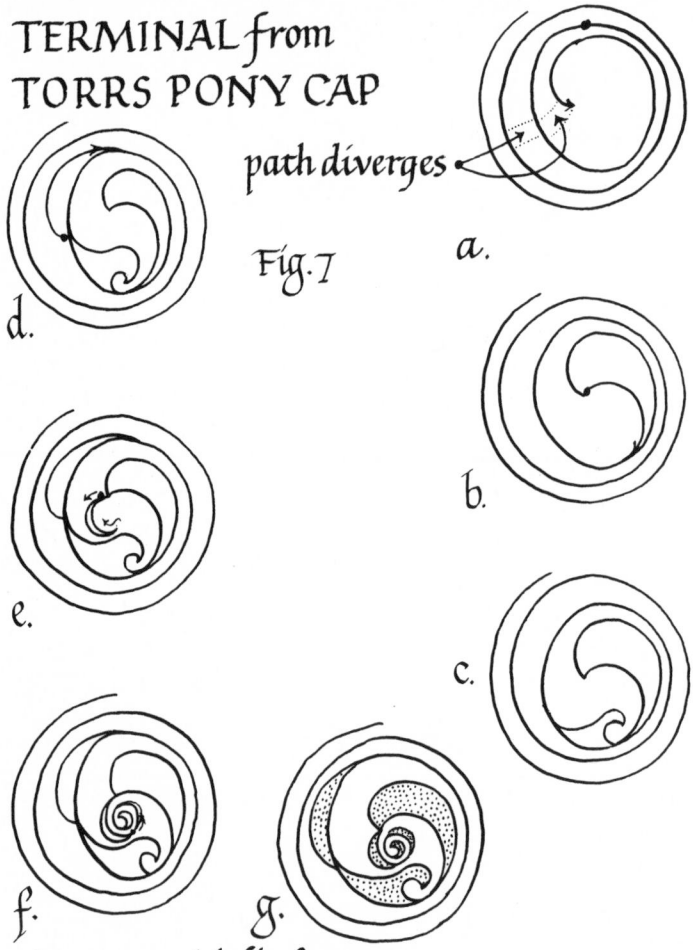


Fig. 7

*Compare with fig. 8, opp.*

a "*labrys*", but as the labrys has many other forms, I shall call this one "*the apple-core*".

One of the earliest forms of the duck-head appears in the N. British school of Celtic metal work that produced the Torrs Pony Cap, about 250 B.C. The basic design may be drawn in one continuous stroke as shown in *fig. 7, a–d*.

*Fig. 8*

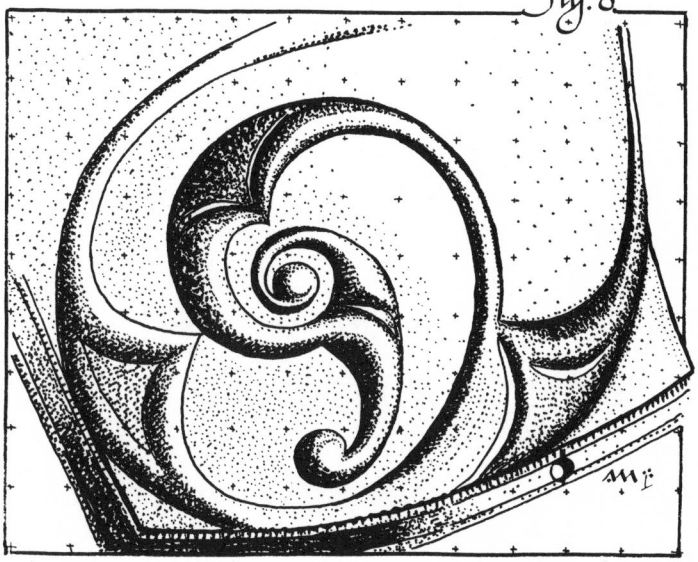

Fig. 8 shows a detail from the Torrs Pony Cap. The design is the prototype of spiral roundels that reach their fullest flowering 1000 years later in the Book of Kells. Modern Celtic artists wishing to develop the tradition further should first grasp the essentials of the art by a close study of the earliest forms such as underlie the later developments.

Fig. 9

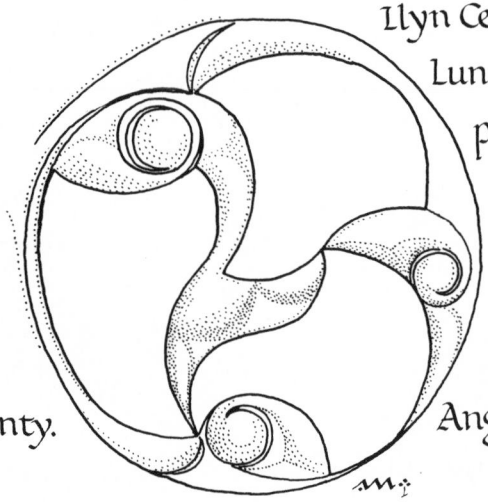

Llyn Cerrig Lunula plaque: Anglesey. 1st. centy. B.C.

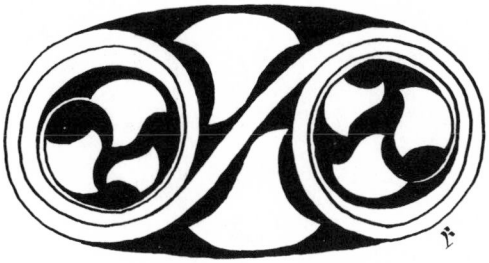

Fig. 10

Fig. 10, for example, seems to be a complete departure from the tradition, but in fact, it is based on the Ilyn Cerrig roundel, Fig. 9. The pattern here is based on petal shapes, freely drawn and randomly grouped. The petal comes from the shape between the spirals in the basic s-scroll, Fig. 11.

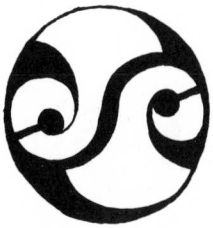

Fig. 11
From circular box lid,
La Tène period, 1st. cent. B.C.,
Cornalaragh, Co. Monaghan.

Fig.12

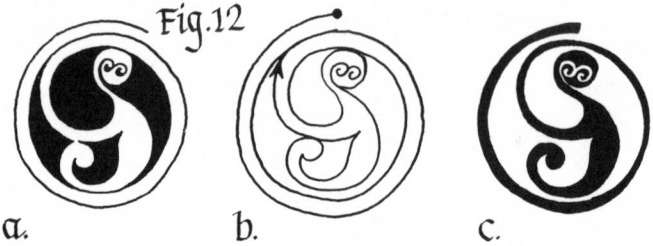

a. b. c.

F.12, duck-head type terminal, Torrs Pony Cap. Background and fore-ground are interchangable, f.12,a,c. Single stroke construction also shown at f.12,b.

Fig.13.

a.

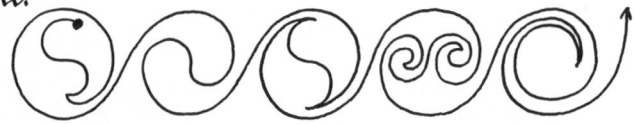

b.

Fig.14

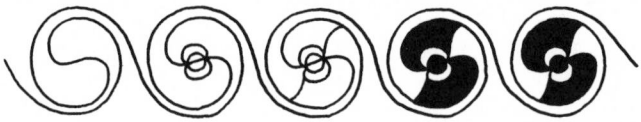

The single line construction appears in this design from Balmaclellan, Kircudbrightshire, c. 30 A.D., f. 13, 14. This is also a series of double spirals, ending in a single spiral, extreme right, f. 13. See also the border below, which starts and ends in single spirals, f. 15.

Fig.15

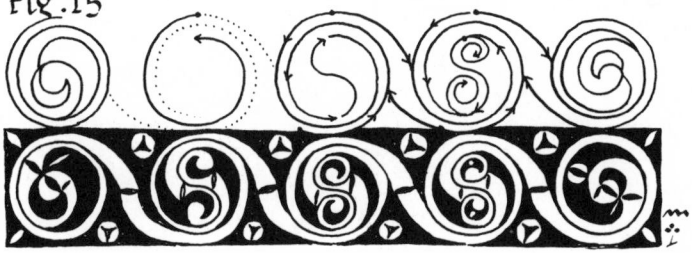

Double spirals in an s-scroll oval, or "cartouche".

Fig 16.

a.

b.

c.

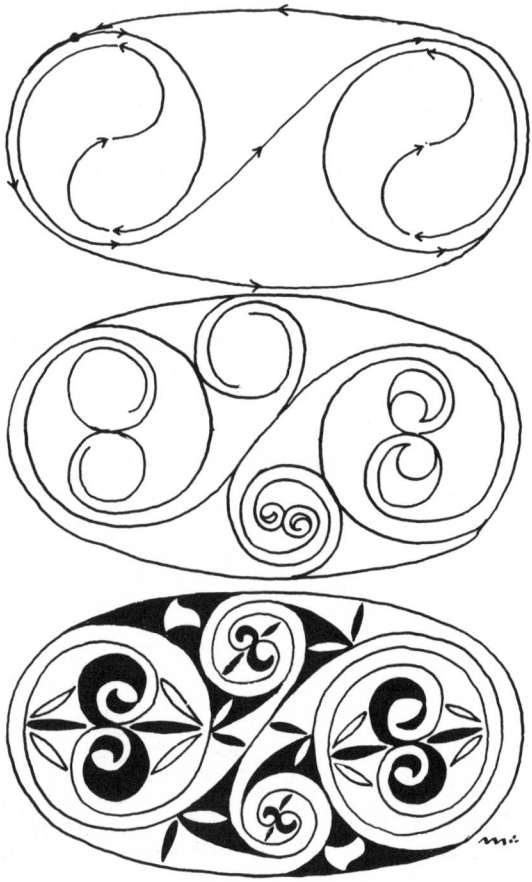

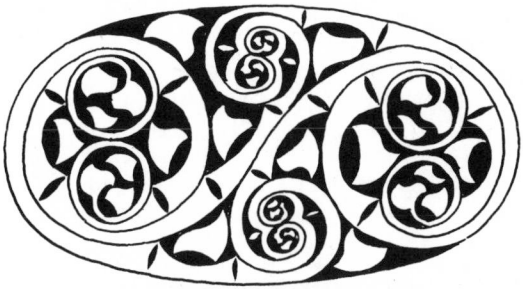

Fig. 17

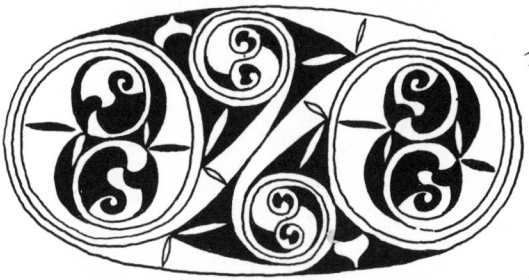

Fig. 18

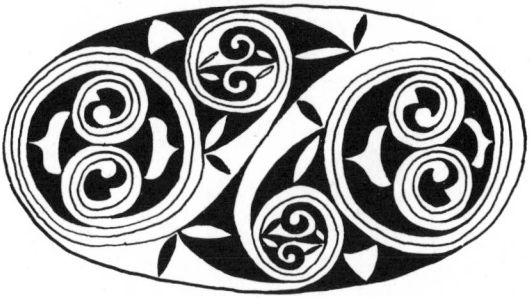

Fig. 19

Compare f. 17 with f. 10; and compare f.s. 18, 19 with f. 13.

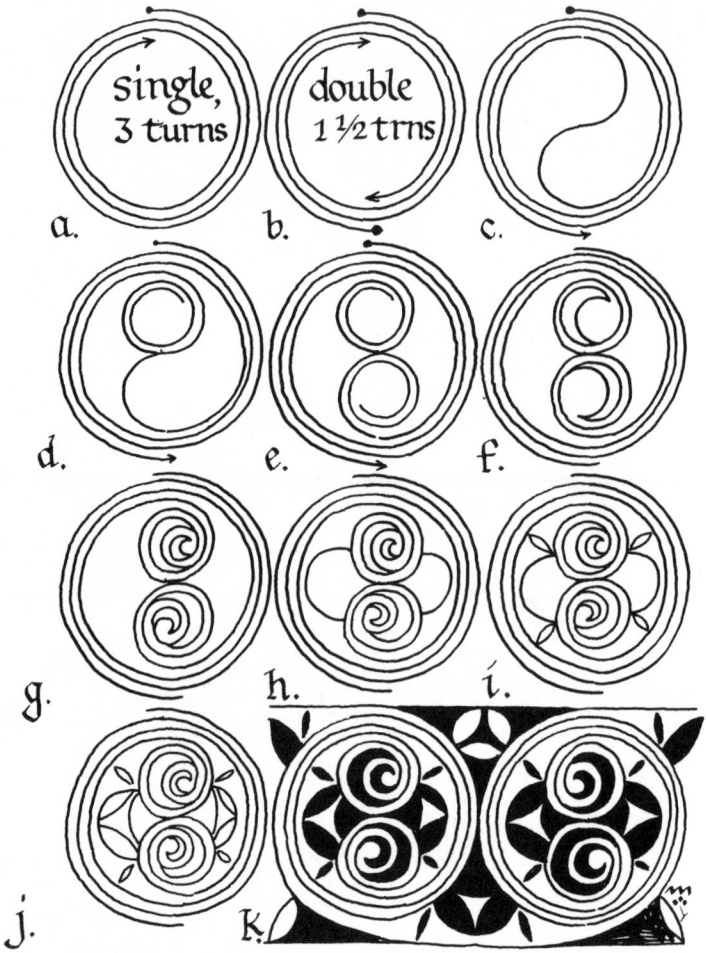


Fig.20 Double spirals, "c-scroll".

# Early Celtic Spirals

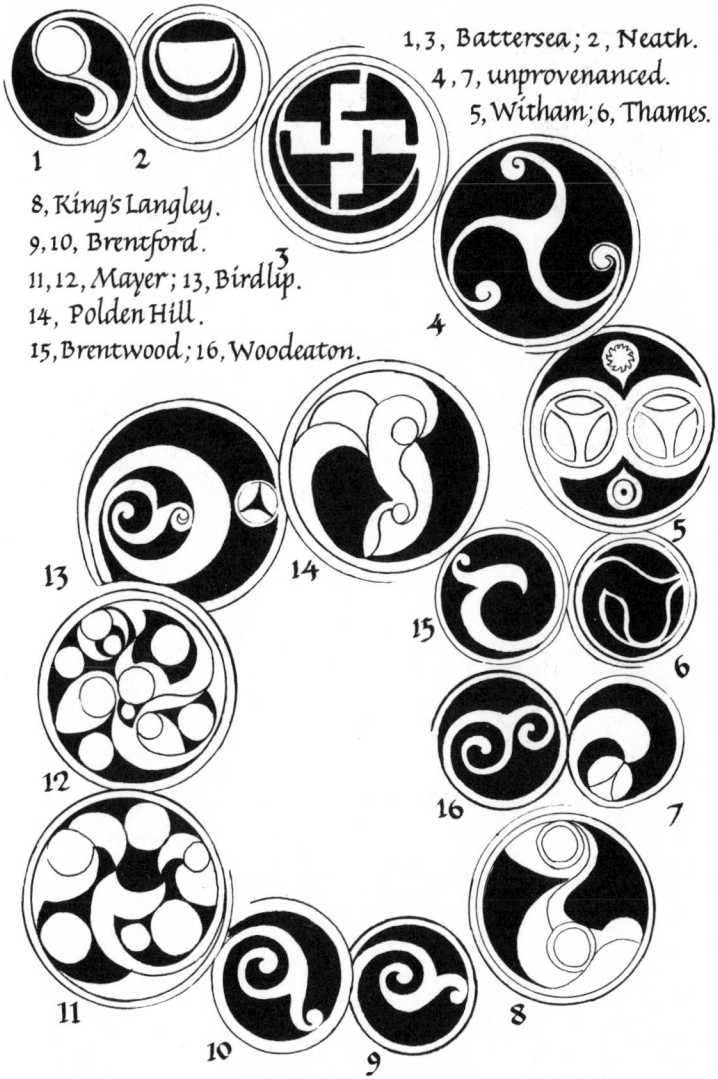

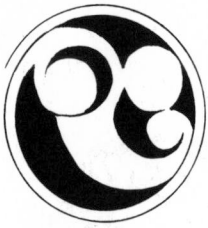

1. Thames

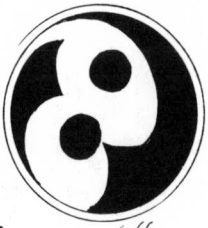

2. polden hill

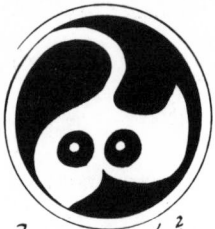

3. Dolphintail ?

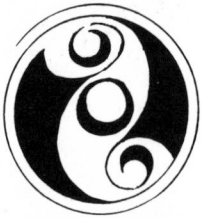

4. Neath, Birdlip

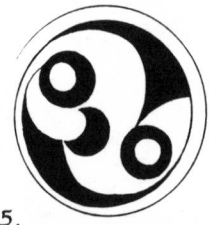

5. Nijmegan

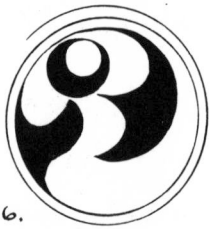

6. Nijmegan

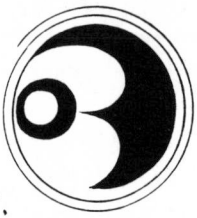

7. Desborough, Birdlip

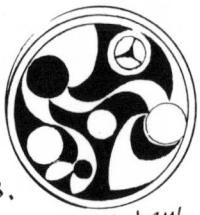

8. Trelan Bahaw

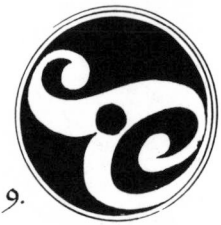

9. Woodeaton

# Early Celtic Spirals

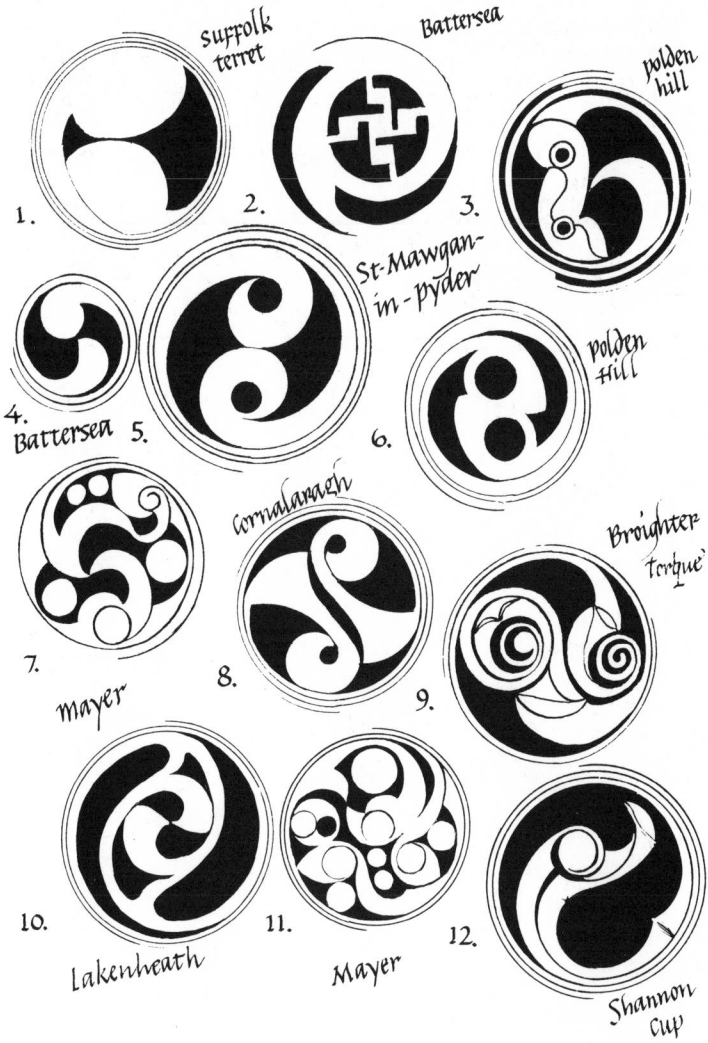

# Geometry of the Spiral

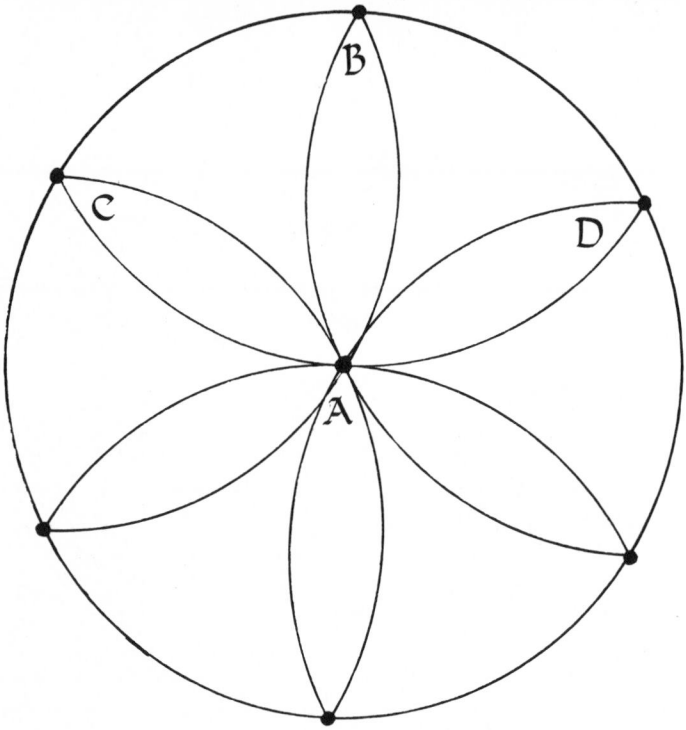

Draw circle, centre A, page 58. With same radius, and centre B, draw arc, C D. Keeping same radius step off the six points, and join in the form of a star as here:

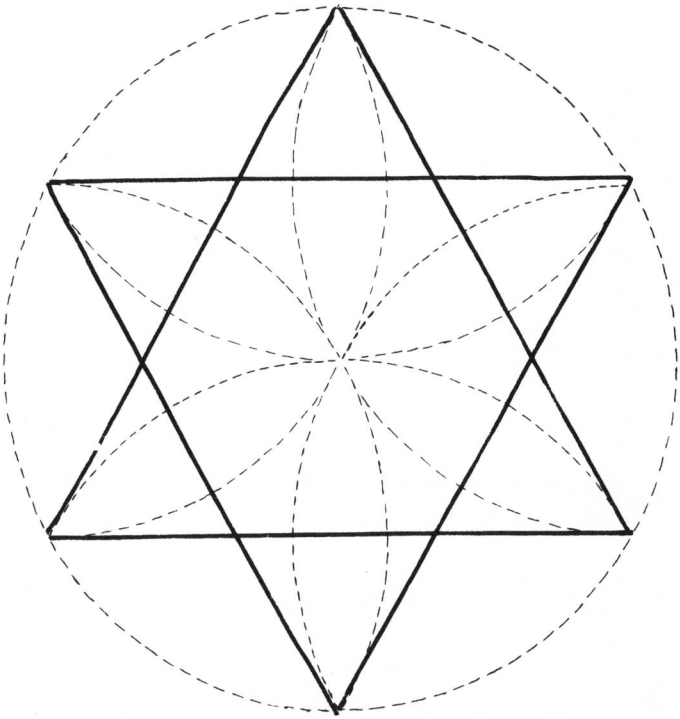

Here the star is used to construct a triangular grid. This grid is used to construct four circles, opposite.

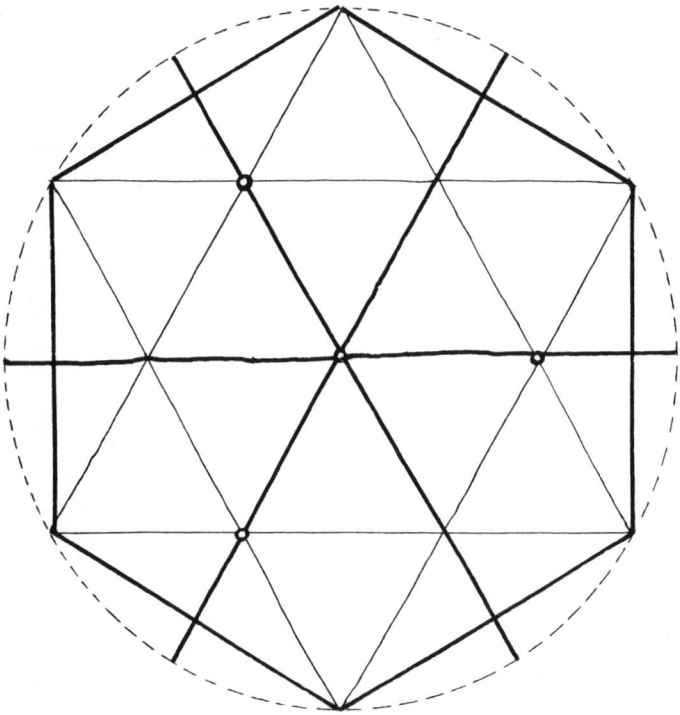

# Geometry of the spiral

The distance between the intersection of the star triangles & the outer hexagon, AB, provides us with the radius for close-packed circles.

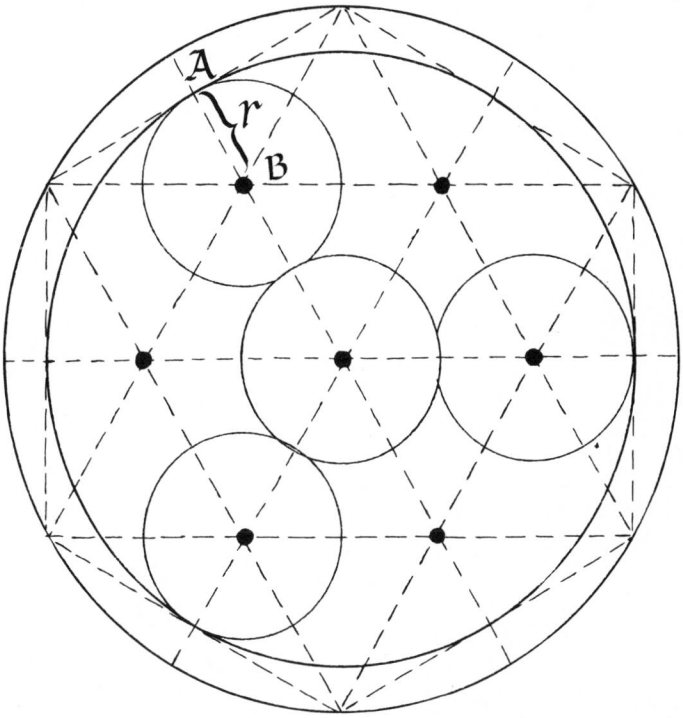

Similarly, seven circles may be packed together.

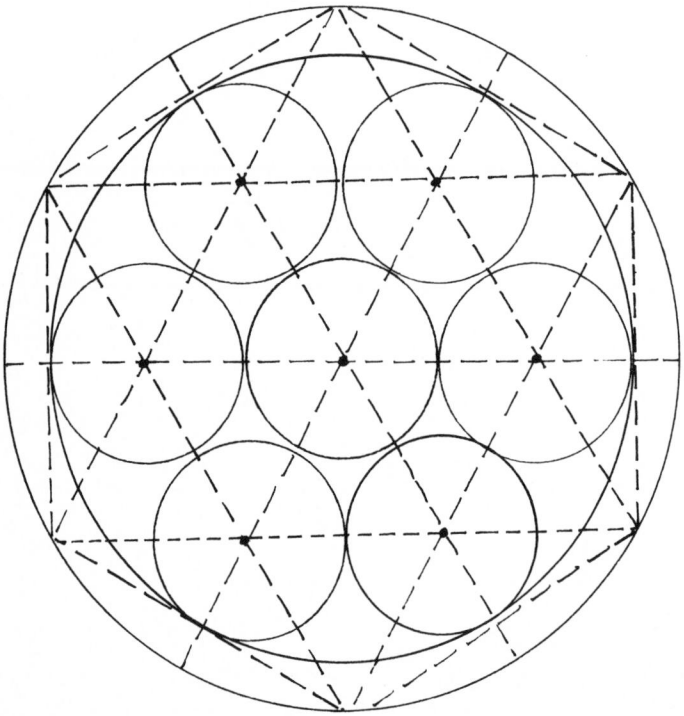

Each circle contains a star. So the whole is reflected in the parts. Triple spirals may be placed in the shaded stars, as will be shown.

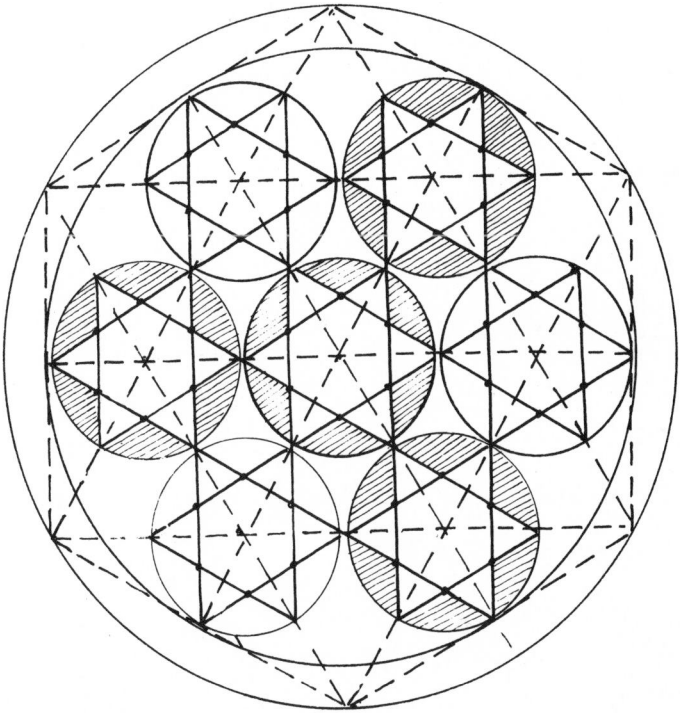

With centres A, B, C
draw arcs DE, FG, HI.
These arcs will connect the triple
spirals.

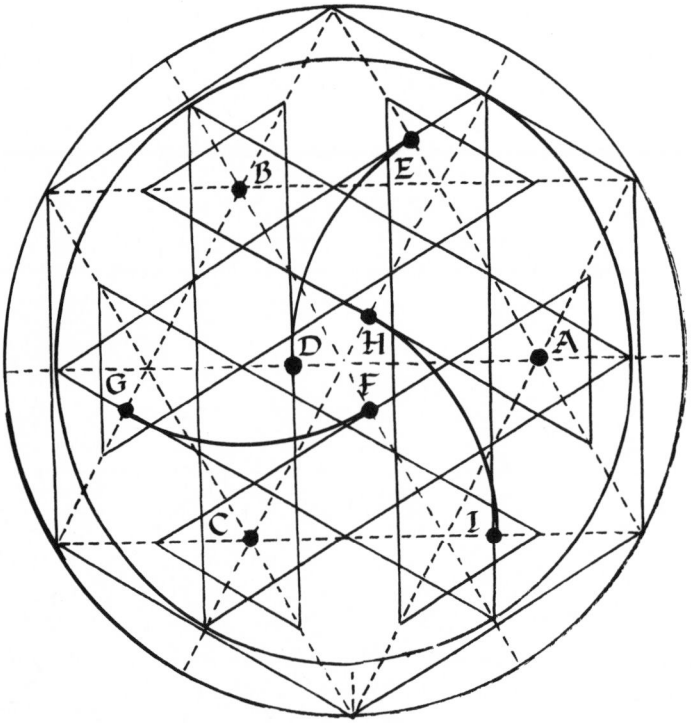

Other arcs, all with radius JK, may be set off from centres J, M, N and O.

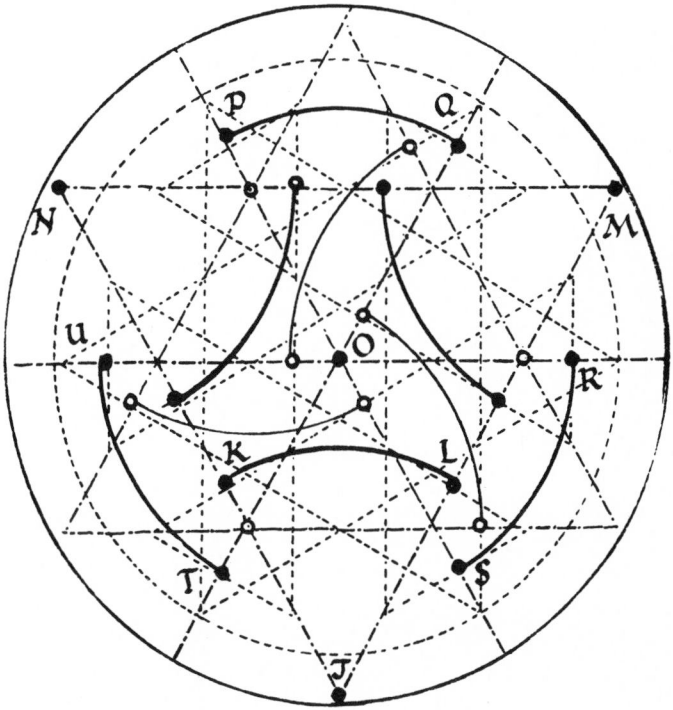

Here the ends of the arcs have been wound into spirals, double and triple. The result is a regular design of continuous line spirals.

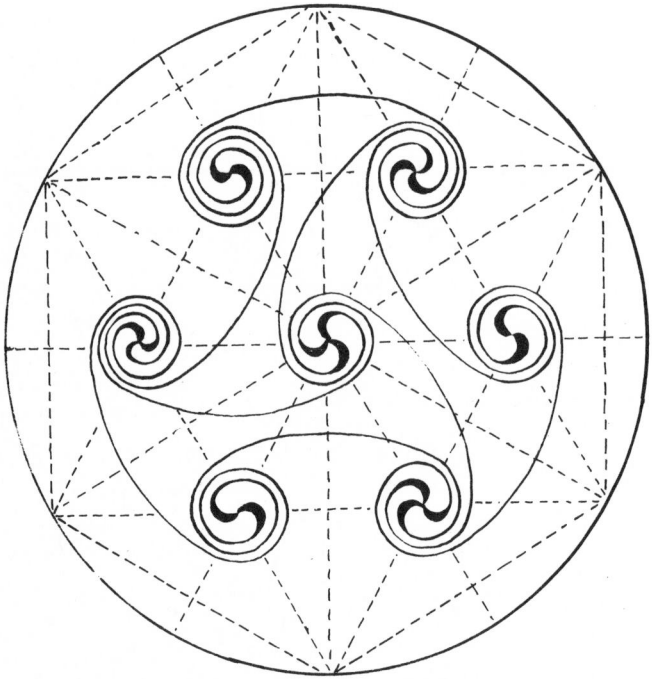

By the addition of three sets of three arcs, the line spirals are converted into interlocking c-scroll paths. The arcs supply bulges in the passages from spiral to spiral.

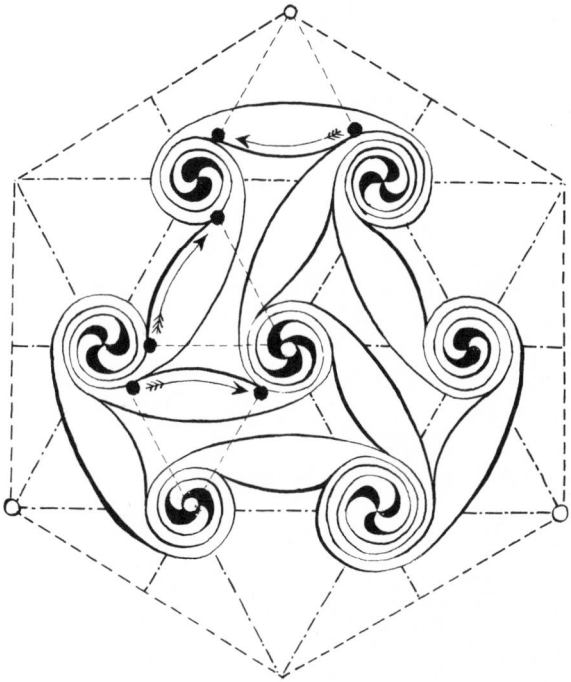

The roundel on the previous page has three double spirals. The addition of one more coil to each of these makes an overall triple spiral, composed of triples, linked together in opposed pairs.

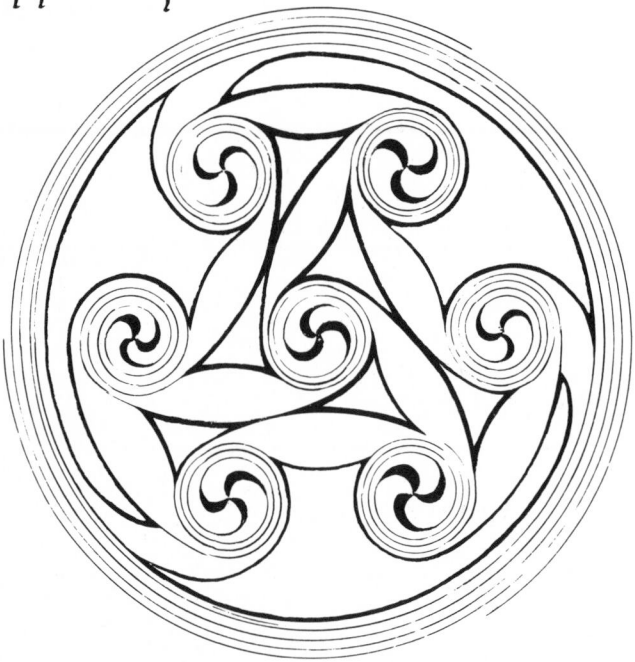

# Geometry of the spiral

As seen above, page 63, the whole is reflected in the parts in the geometry of circle, hexagon & star, the same geometry as generates the triple spiral roundel, opposite and here beneath:

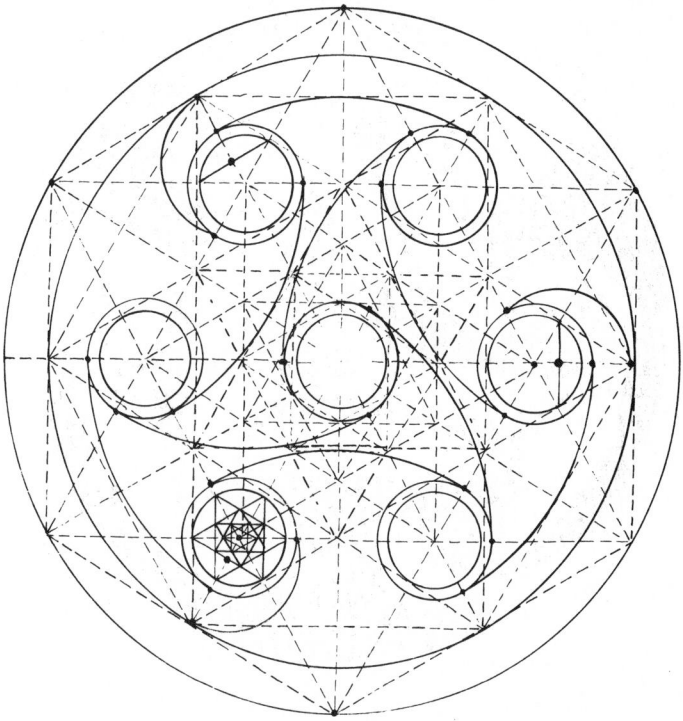

WITH this in view it follows that the whole triple spiral design may be reflected in each of the triples contained within it, thus:

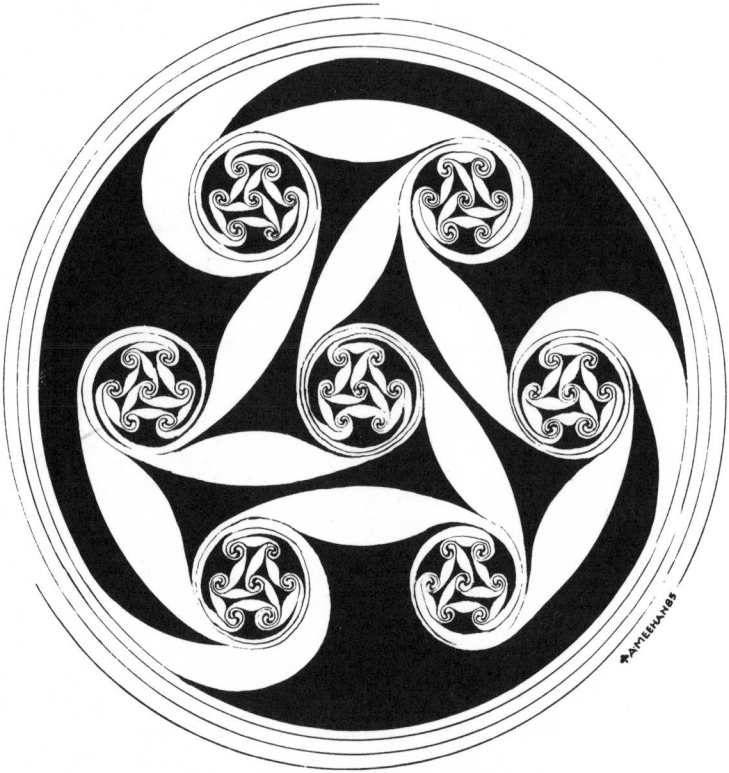

# Chapter V Irish Half Uncial Script

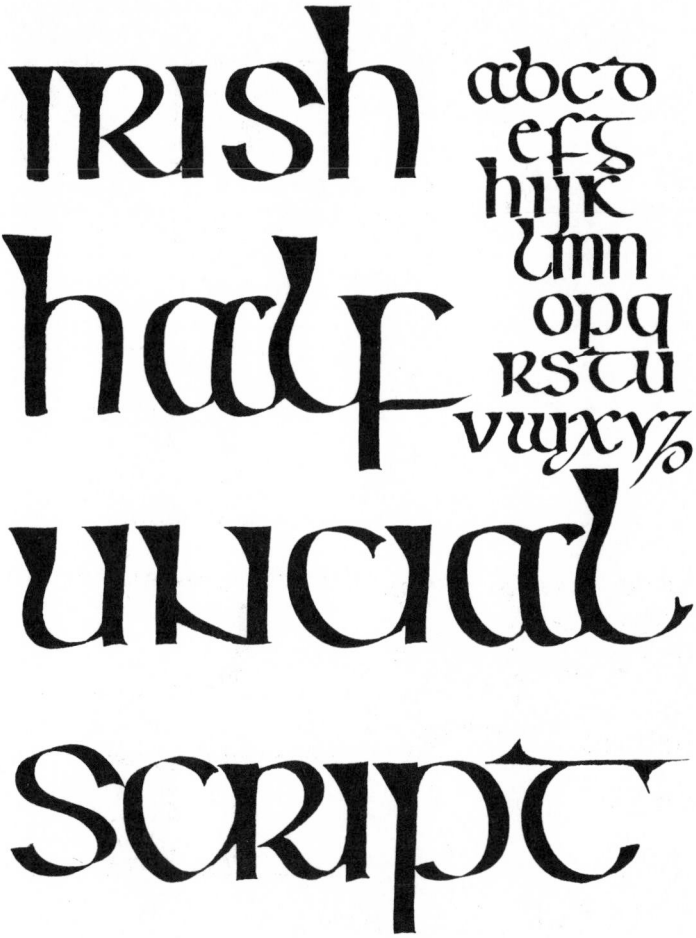


Alphabet written with Speedball nib, C-1.

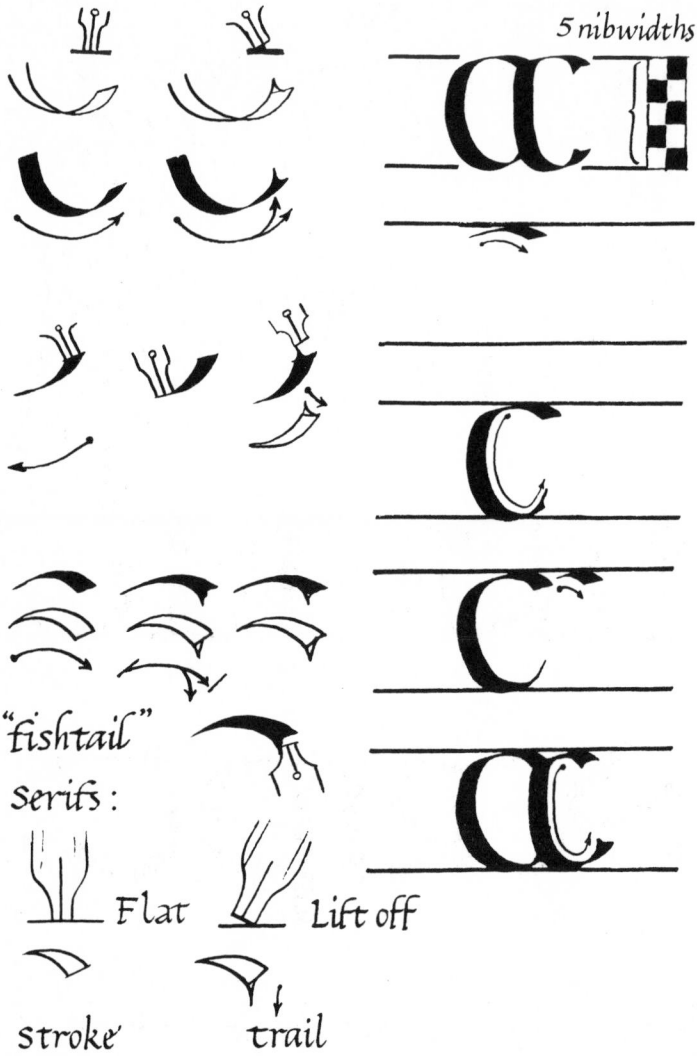
5 nibwidths
"fishtail"
serifs:
Flat
Lift off
stroke
trail

ascender, 2½ nib widths.
"x" height, five n.w's.

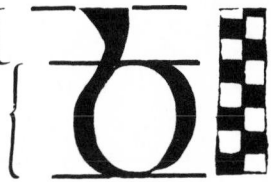

Flag serifs, on tops of straight, vertical strokes only, except for 'b' and 'l', which begin straight, then curve.

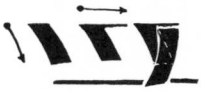

Letters b, upright d, f, h, i, j, k, l, m, n, p, q, r, u, (v), w, (y), all have flag serifs. While Fishtails are optional, flag serifs are not.

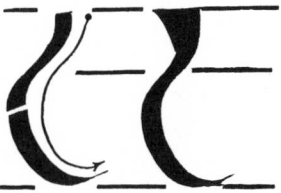

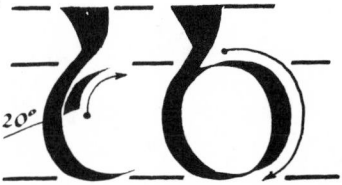


For the most part, except for serif and foot pen-twists, pen angle should approach a 20° constant.

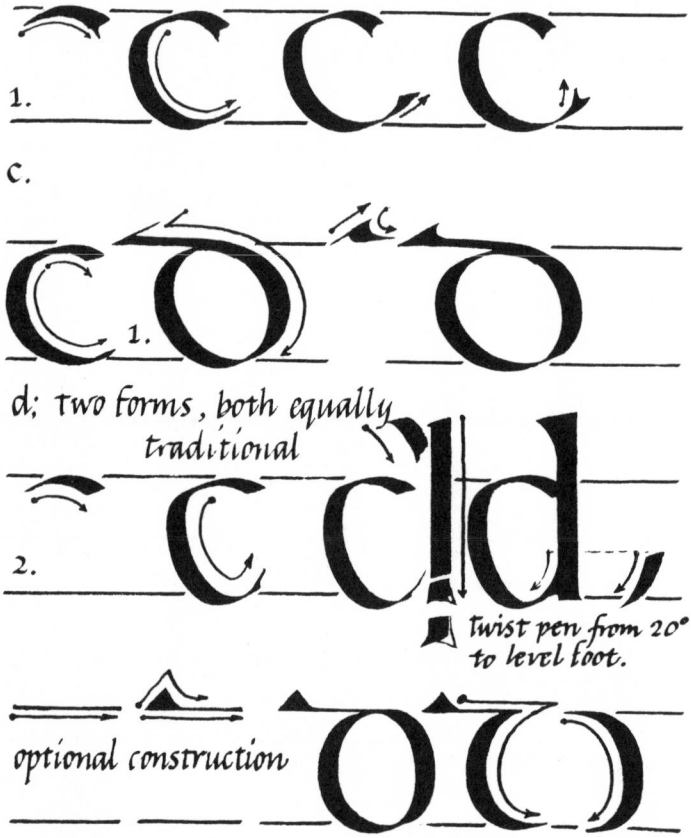


Use one d or another, not both in same text.

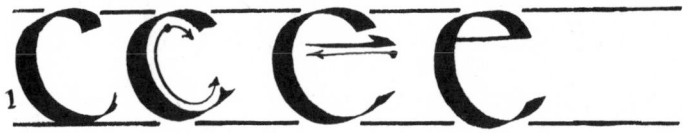


e.

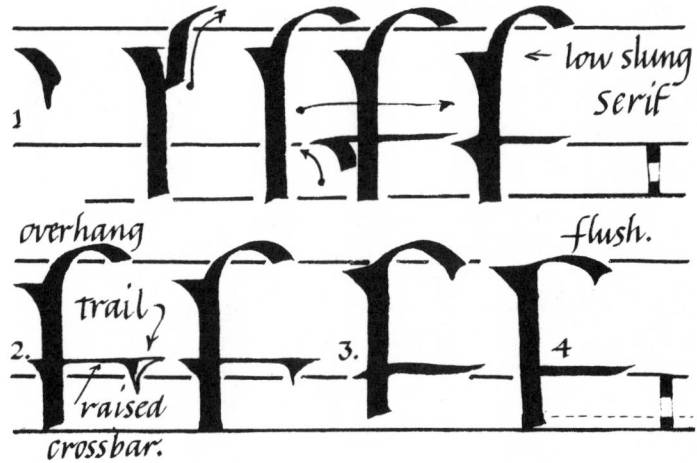


f: several versions, 4 is the most compact.

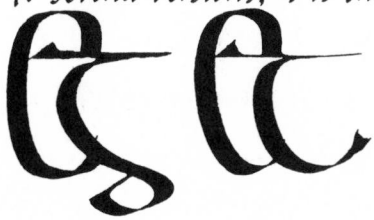

eg, et – this type of tall letter e is used before t and g.

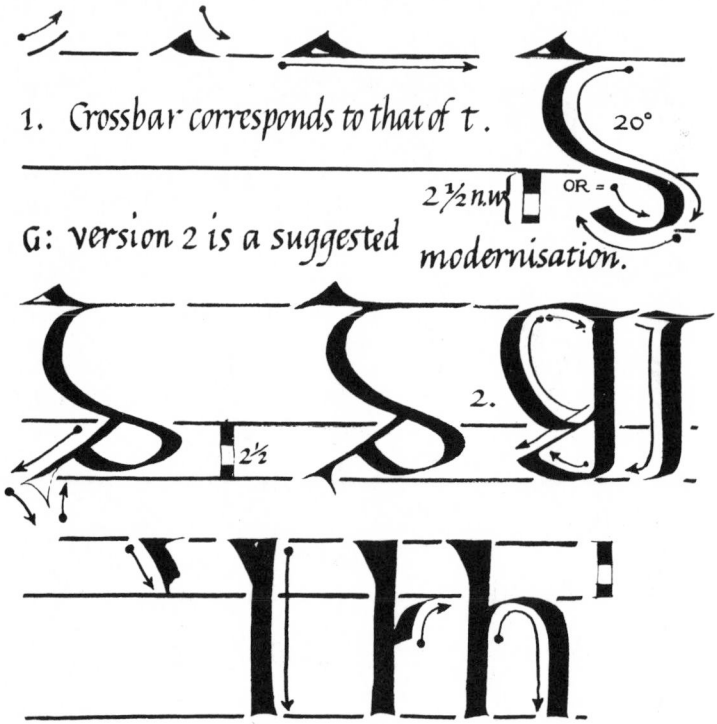


The tail serif on the celtic g may be trailed with the left hand corner of the nib. The modernised form is based on q, below, and may be used with q, 1.

i: the final downstroke may be given a final twist to level the foot from 20°-horizontal.

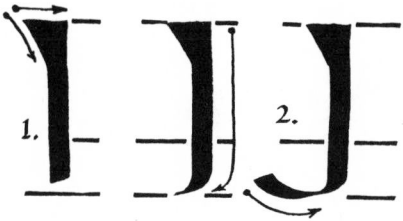


j, 3 variations:

2: a modernised version.

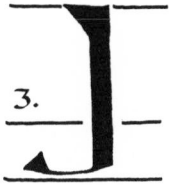


3: this foot is borrowed from that of the letter q, see below.

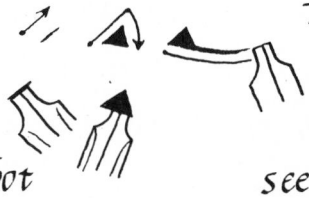

Triangular foot may be drawn by twisting pen, or added on with a small pointed nib, such as a crow-quill.

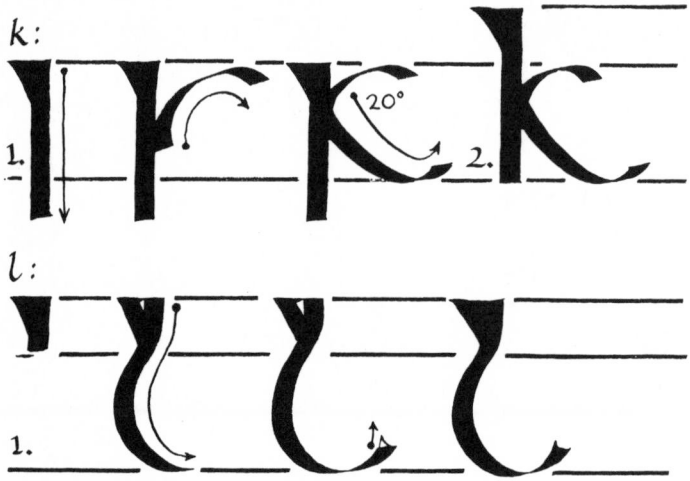


There is no letter k in the original Celtic mss., so one of the challenges is to supply missing letters, j, k, v, w, as well as to modernise the archaic ones, particularly g, q, t, and y. Here the first k is very compatible with the old forms, while k2 is slightly modern looking.

m:

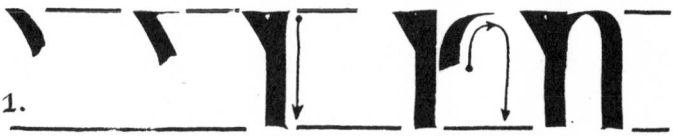


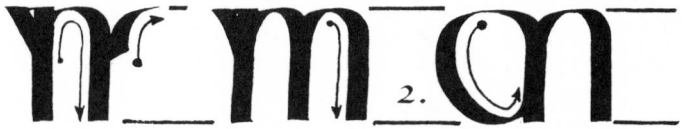


m; two variants, the first is the regular one, the second only for use as the first letter of a word. The point to remember about the letter m is that its arches are much narrow than the arch of n or h.

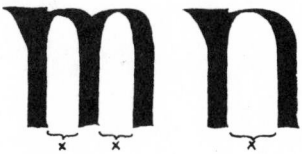

# Chapter V

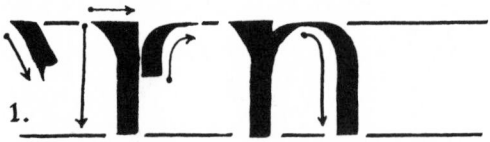


1. This form relates to the letter, h.

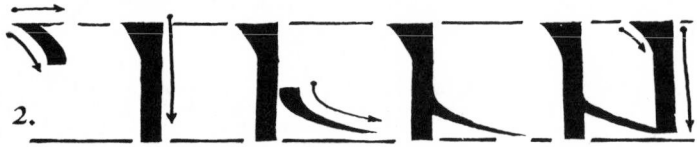


This form is very much a majuscule;

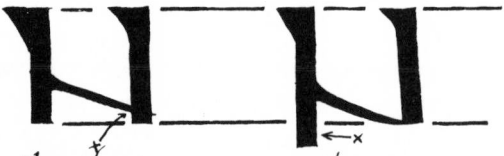

the slant may sometimes come above the right foot; the left foot may descend a little.

These two n's, however, should not be used in the same text. Use one or the other.

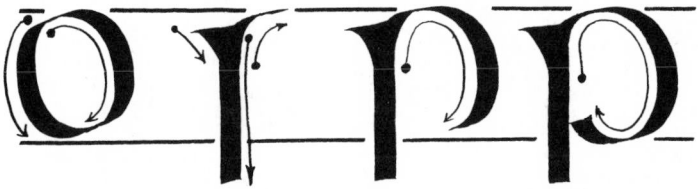

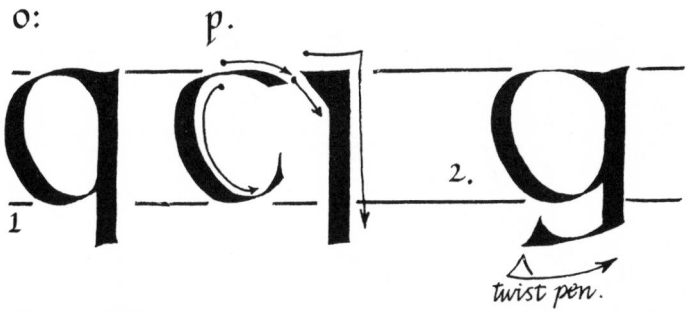


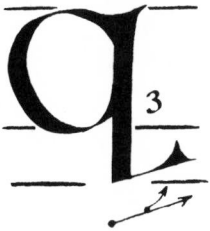


q, 3 variations: the first two are traditional, the third is a modern version, with a reversal of the foot; this last may be used with g, 2, above, as may q, 1.

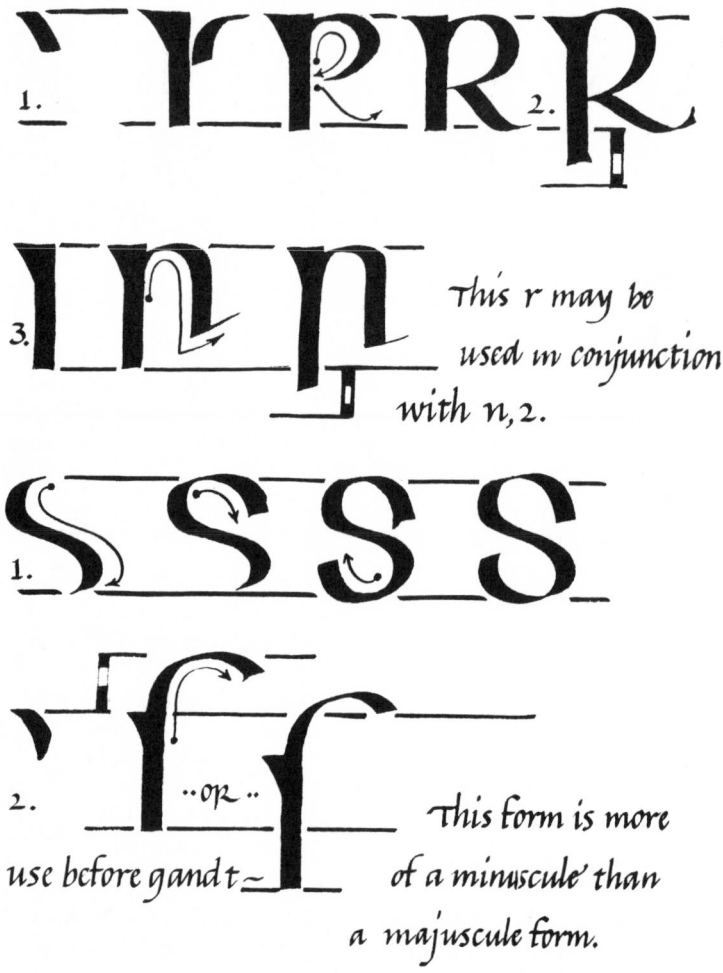
1.
2.
3.
This r may be used in conjunction with n, 2.
1.
2.
..or..
This form is more of a minuscule than a majuscule form.
use before g and t

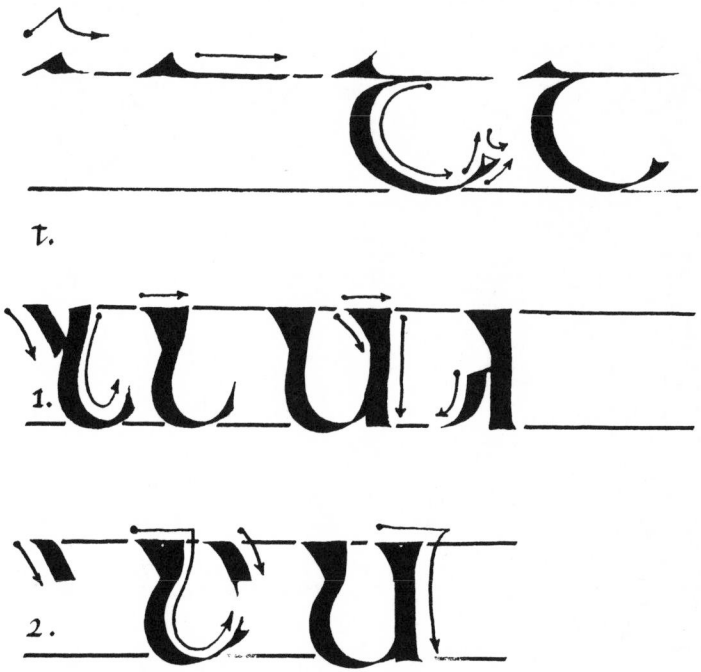


The difference between u, 1 and 2 is that the first is pulled straight from the serif into the curve; the second bends to the left, rather than being pulled down straight.

# Chapter V

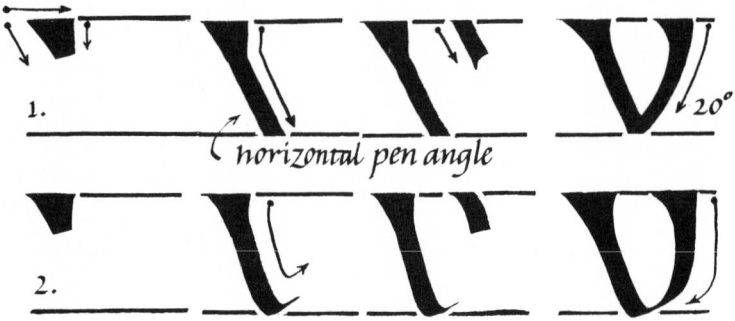


V: two variations: these are suggestions only.

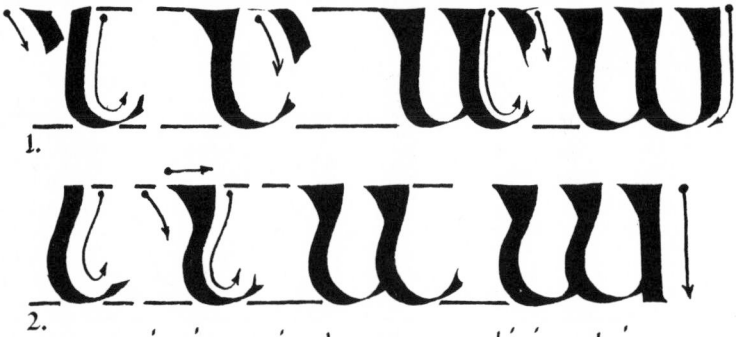


W: variation 2 is the more traditional in style.

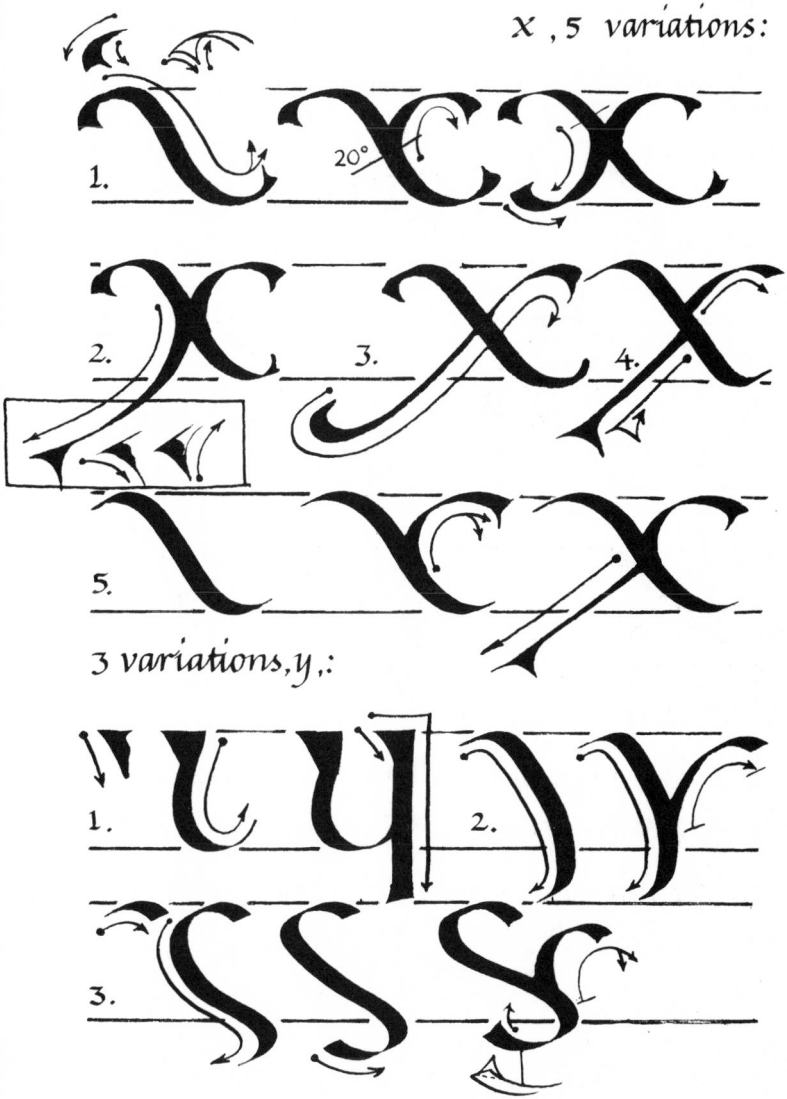
x , 5 variations:
1.
20°
2.
3.
4.
5.
3 variations, y,:
1.
2.
3.

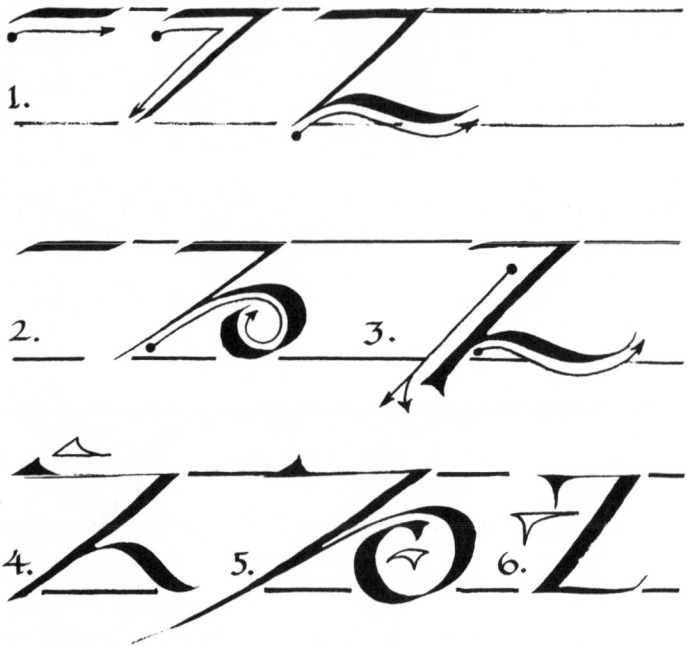


z : like many of the letters in this alphabet, z allows for a number of mutations, whereby the pen may be given free play. Here, 3, 4, 6 are variants of 1, while 5 is a variant of 2.

# HOW TO LAY OUT A MANUSCRIPT PAGE

ONCE YOU are familiar with the letters of any particular script it is best to select a text and produce a single-page manuscript, or a number of such pages. A text may be written over many times, and may be improved a little each time; you can develop a sense of design by doing this, and produce work that truly pleases you, that you may include in your portfolio, or present, suitably matted and mounted of course, to a friend.

# Chapter VI

FIRST you need a lot of paper. It need not be very special but it is worth getting a batch of good, non-acid, not too thin, smooth, white paper. 2-ply "Bristol board" does quite well. Stock up with 50 or 100 sheets from an art supplies outlet. A good size is 36"x 28". Store paper flat, wrapped up safe from damp, dust, pawmarks, and such. A closet may be adapted to paper storage by putting in shelves.

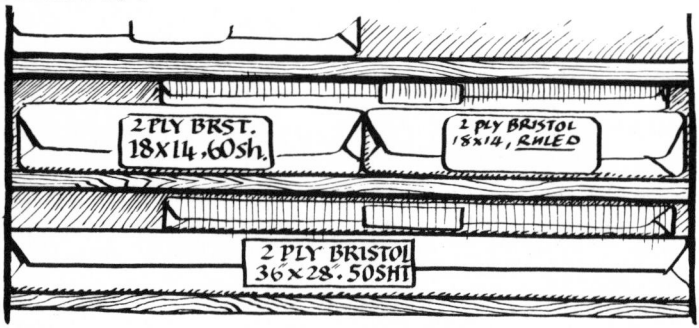

WHEN you buy a stock of paper in a whole or broken packet, keep it in its wrapper until ready to use. Remove as many sheets as you need, close up the remainder and return to storage. Keep the sheets in the same order as they came from the package, same face up, same corner alignment. Pencil lightly a mark in the upper left hand corner, to help keep the sheets in order. One side of the paper, for instance, is sometimes better than the other to write on, and you will want to find out which before ruling up your single pages, so as to stack the pages with the better side up.

## MEASURING THE PAPER FOR CUTTING

TAKE ONE SHEET & MEASURE IT 18" along one side, 14" the other. If your sheet is 36"x28" to begin with, it will quarter economically to a standard 18"x14" page; if not, trim it down.

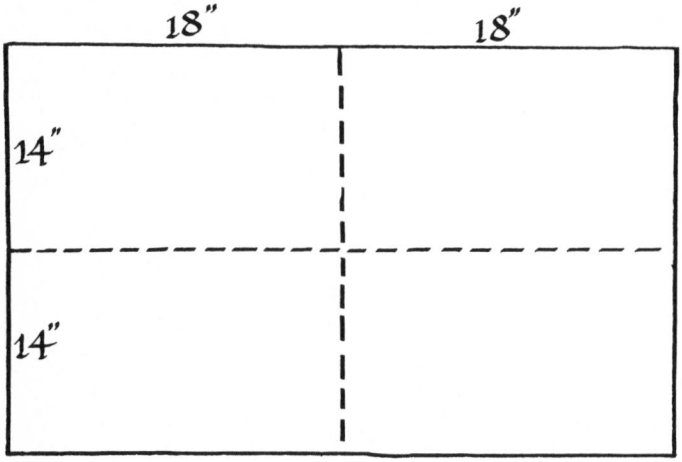

## MARKING THE CUTTING MAT.

TRIMMING A LOT OF PAGES may be done more easily on a cutting mat, a sheet of dense card or illustration board at least ⅛" thick, 4' x 3'. On this, pencil the 36" x 28" area, divide each side and quarter the area. Having checked the lines and angles, ink in the marks for the corners and the cuts to be made.

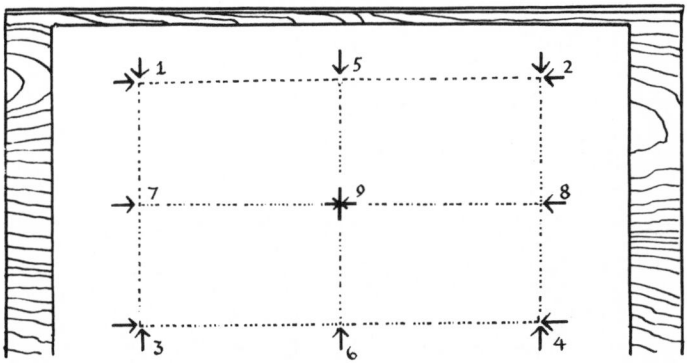

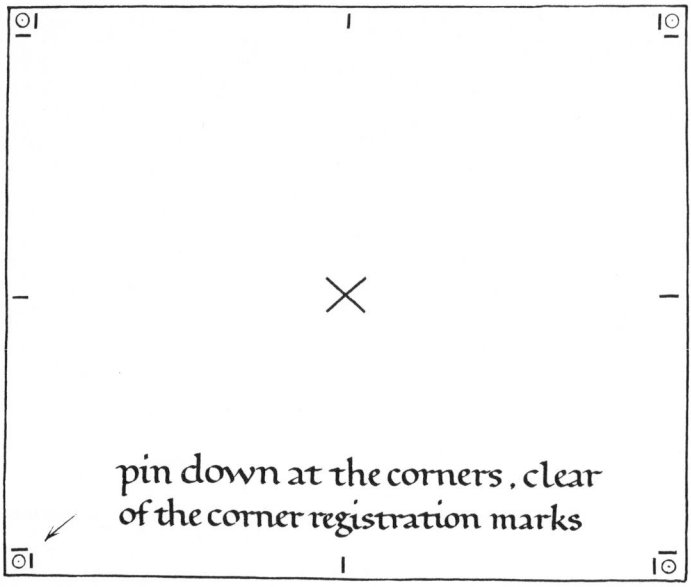


TAKE THE CUTTING MAT, marked up as illustrated above; lay it on a board, and pin it down. For the board, a sheet of plywood, 4' x 3', will do – get the lumber yard to cut down an 8' x 4' sheet to a couple of boards; both will prove handy to have about the studio.

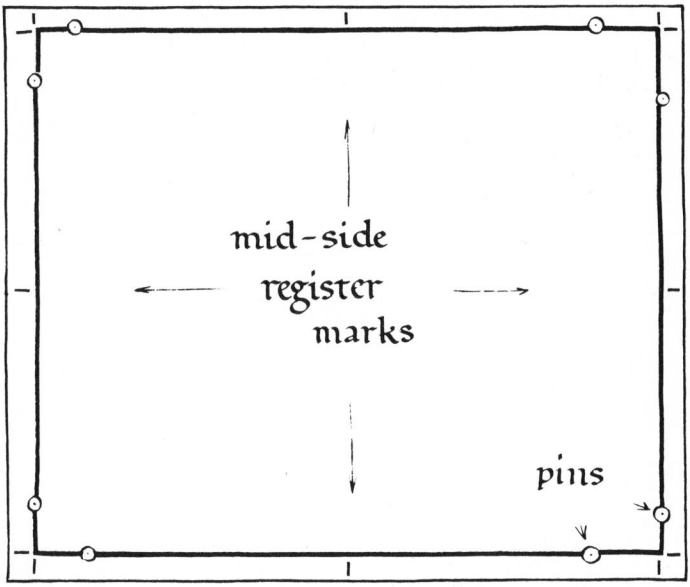


NOW TAKE A NUMBER OF sheets; squared up, stacked and lined up on the cutting mat with the corner registration marks. Pin down the stack with old-fashioned, large-headed drawing pins; pin clear of the register marking the mid-point of each side.

When you pin the stack of pages, do not pierce the paper with the shaft of the pin. The head of the pin only should hold the paper. The bigger the pin-head, the better.

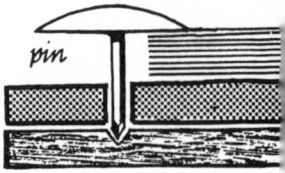


The sort of blade you snap off is very handy.

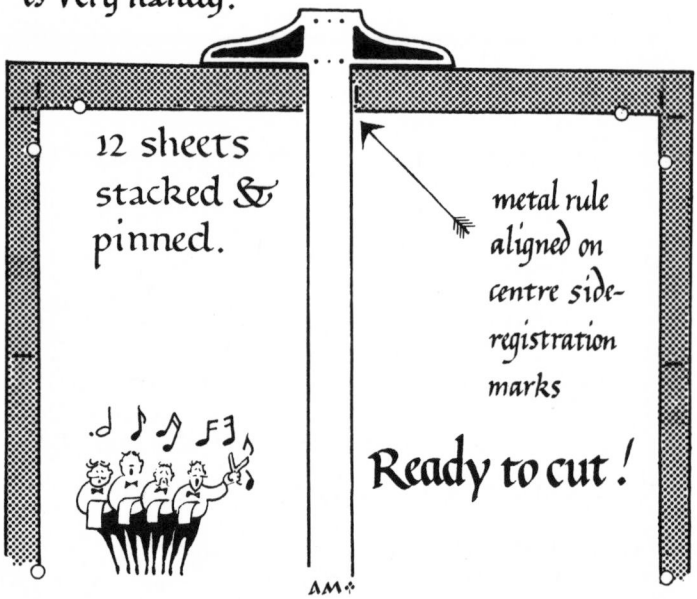

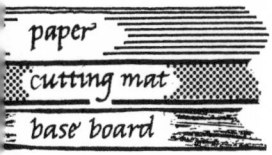


Never use a wood or plastic edged ruler when cutting; a metal edged or all-metal ruler is a must for all cutting jobs.

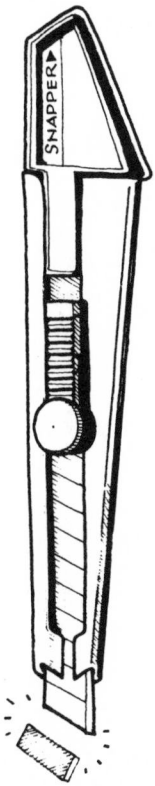


When cutting, press down on the ruler with one hand, but do not press on the knife any more than is needed to cut through a single sheet at a time, for the most accurate result. Remove the cut sheets one by one.

Make the first cut from top to bottom. Then cut from side to side, according to the registration marks. Snap off the blade, half-way through.

NOW YOU HAVE CUT A dozen sheets, 36"x 28", into four dozen pages, 14"x 18", or an ample supply of standard-size stock of paper suitable for single-page manuscript, enough to last a year.

You also have your studio equipped to handle most cutting jobs. The board and mat set-up will be reused as is. Store it flat against the wall until it is needed again.

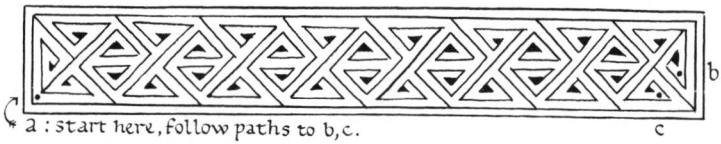

NEXT the page must be ruled for writing, but ruling can become tiresome and off-putting, whereas a number of pages may be ruled all at the same time by means of a simple template.

## HOW TO MAKE A TEMPLATE FOR RULING

RULE one sheet first, in pencil, according to the plan illustrated on the next page. This is the master lay out for the template, and therefore should be made as carefully as can be. Check the corners and the intersections with the T-square and set square to be sure the right angles are true.

THE RULES' spacing given here is standardised to the proportions of a nib width of 1/16".

We will use a Celtic script, of which the letter 'o' is five nib widths high. The rules are three 'o's' apart, or 15/16".

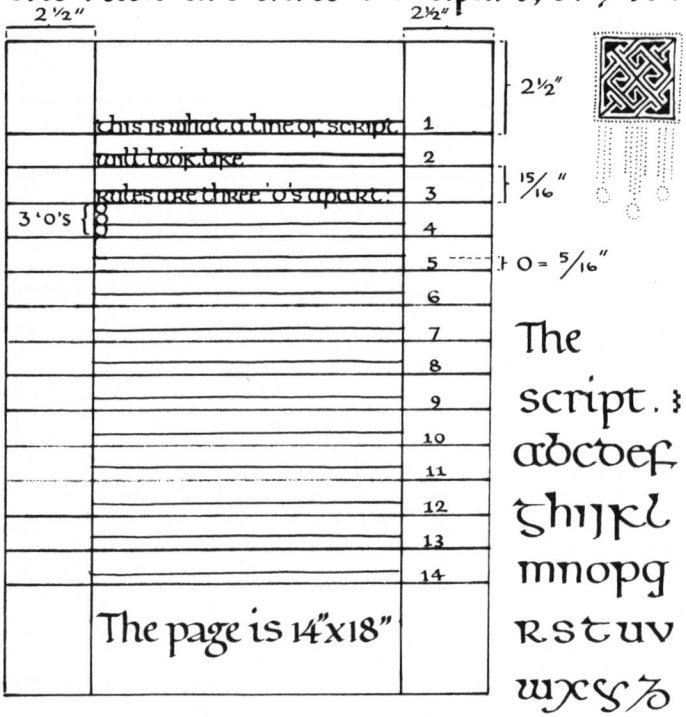

WHEN you have this page all ruled up, you can use it to rule up a number of other pages, as a template. To make the template, with a pin, prick holes through the page where the rules for the lines cross the margins. With a pencil you can transfer the points on to a second sheet placed directly beneath the template. Removing the template, the second sheet may be ruled up according to the transferred guide points. Likewise, the template may be re-used to rule any number of single-page manuscript pages.

Or, with a fine, strong pin, you may prick through several sheets at once.

# How to Decorate Letters

## I, n, o, ë, and l

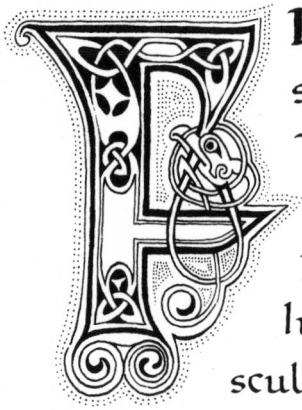

FIRST OF ALL WE NEED some letters to decorate. They may be drawn, as on the following pages. Here I have simplified the old Irish letters, called Majuscules, and presented them in a proportion which is based on a $5^2$ grid.

All the letter forms on these pages are intended as models for drawing the outlines of outsize letters to be illuminated with Celtic ornament.

I have given the grid as based on a square divided into five on each side, or 5x5, because I have found this to have had special significance to early illuminators, such as those of the Lindisfarne Gospels. Also, this gives a good proportion between the width of the stroke and height, as of the letter 'I', for instance: 1/5. With the addition of the outline, this proportion approximates the Lindisfarne ideal nibwidth: i-height, 1:4½.

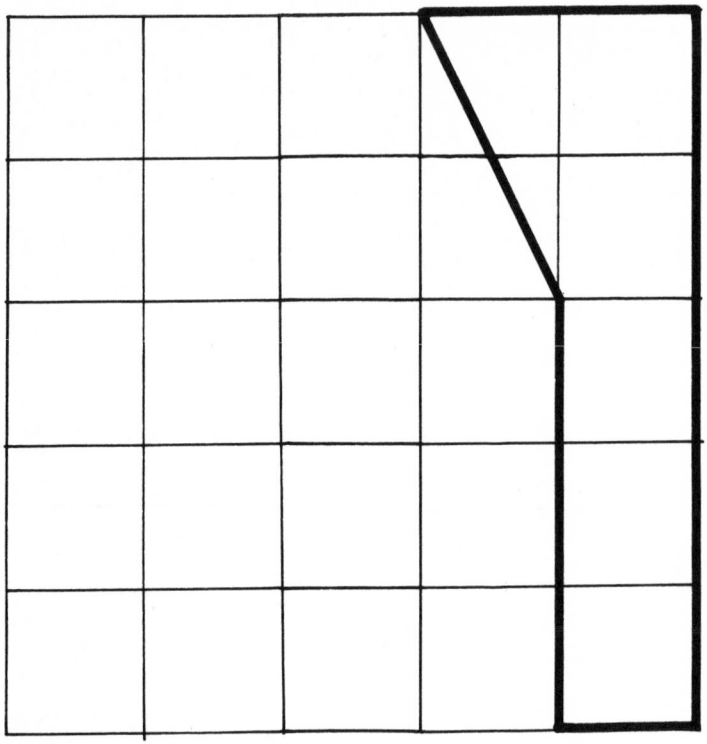

The side of the square is the height of the letter 'I', as here, or width of an 'O', page 109, below. If it were pen-written, it would be 5 nib widths high.

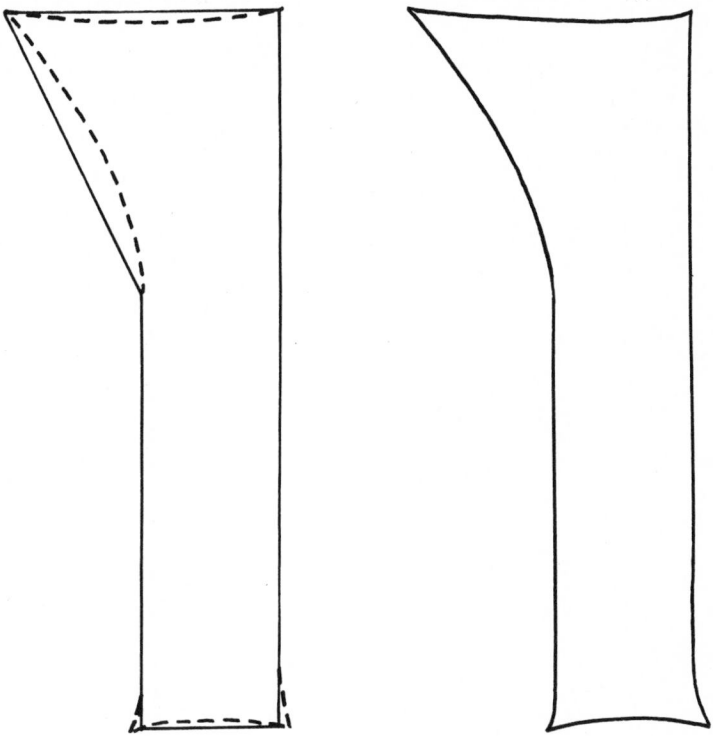

The grid gives us a standard proportion for majuscules, as well as the ideal flag serif. The angles may curve a little, as here.

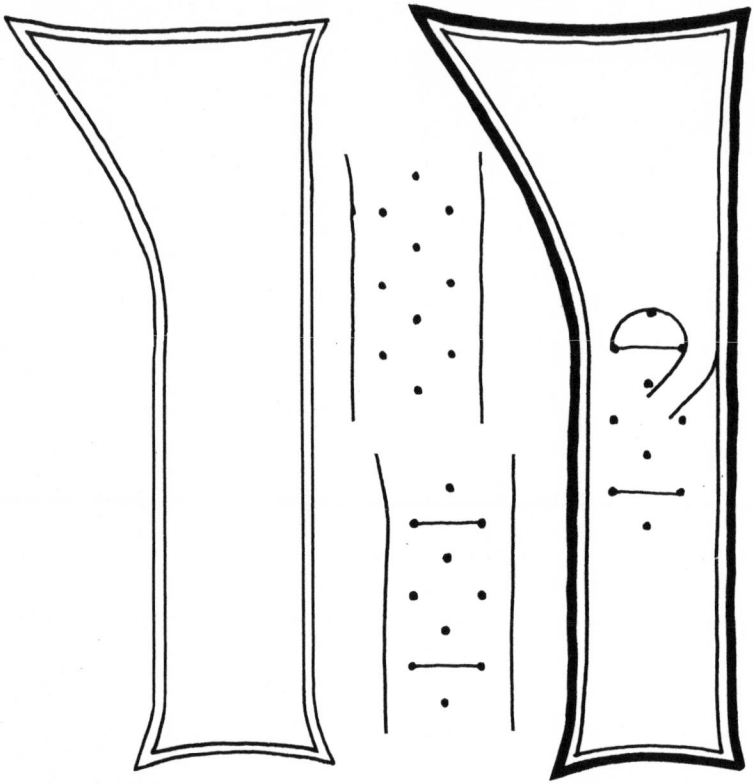

Outline the letter; thicken up the outline; add another outline. Colour the interior lightly and brightly ~ or put in a knot.

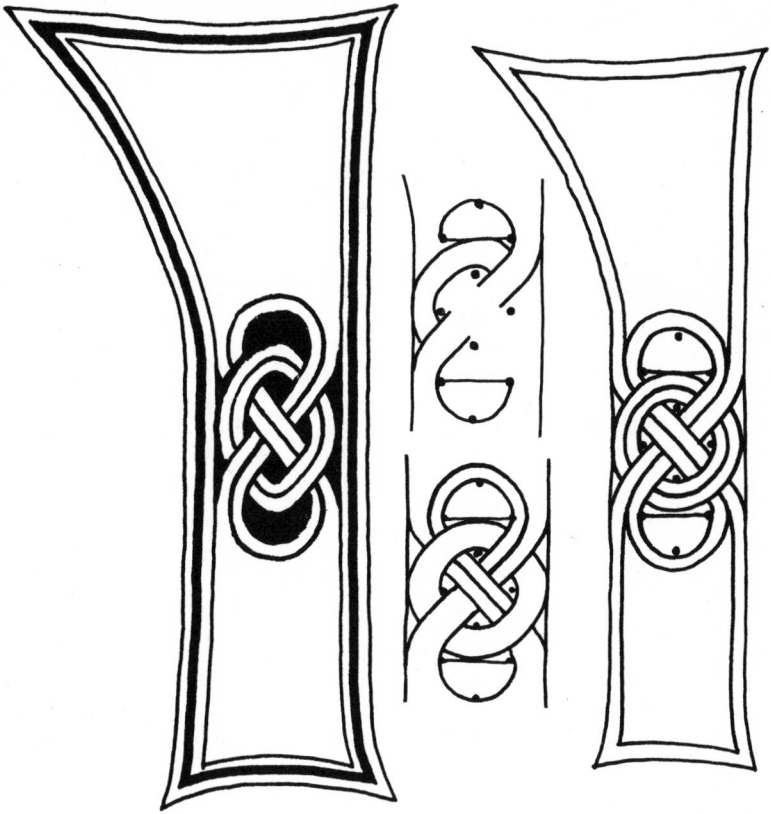

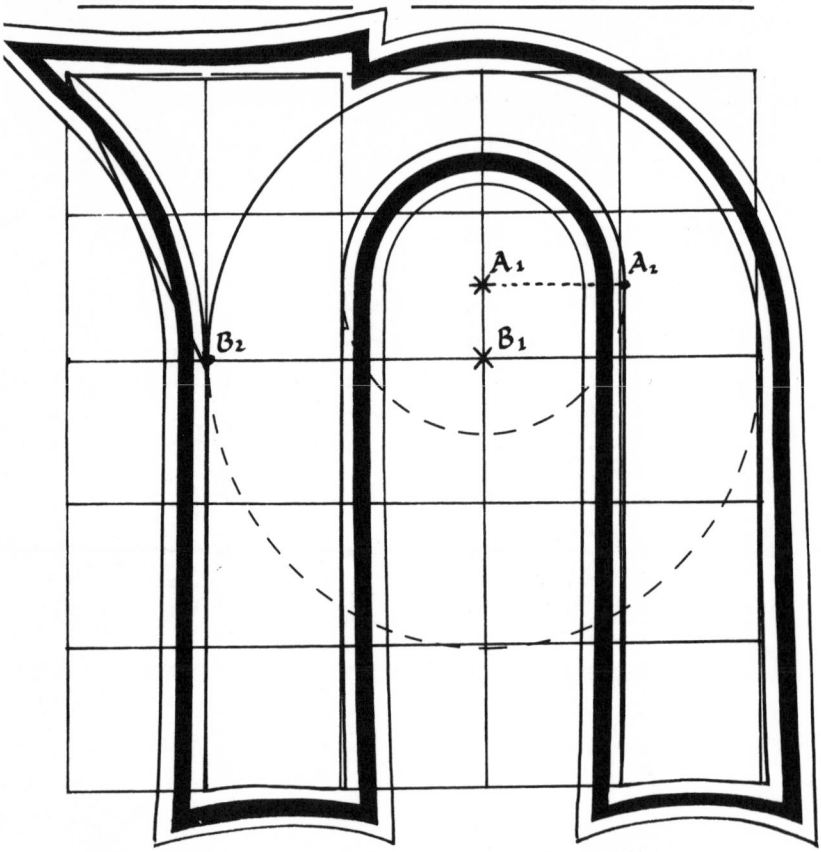


After I, the letter N may be analysed on a 5² grid. This figure may be followed as a model in free-hand drawing, or as a geometric

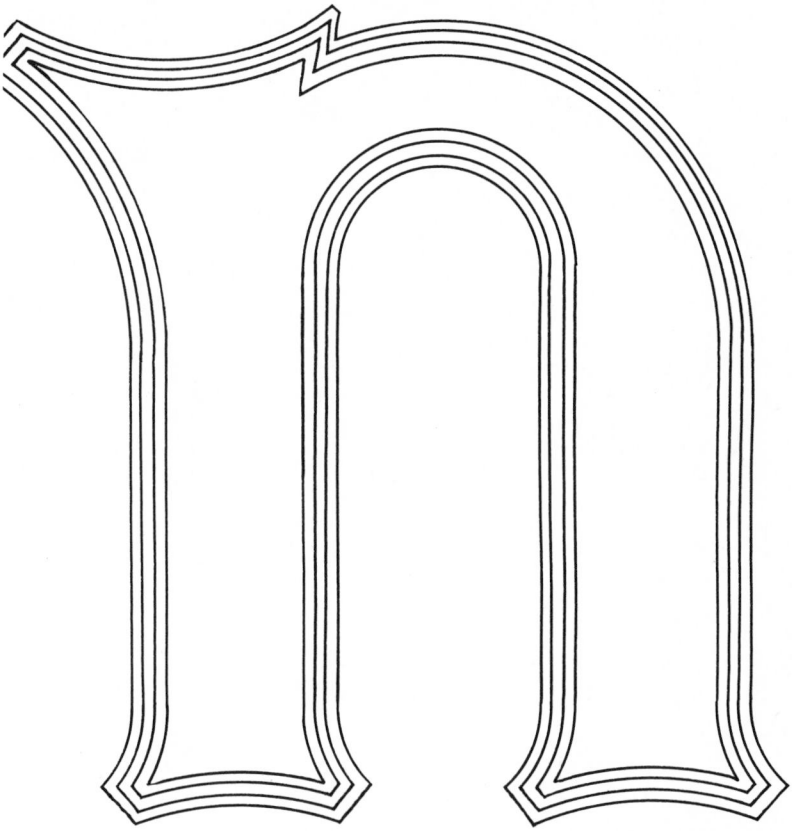

exercise. With compasses and ruler the entire letter may be produced. The centre band may be coloured.

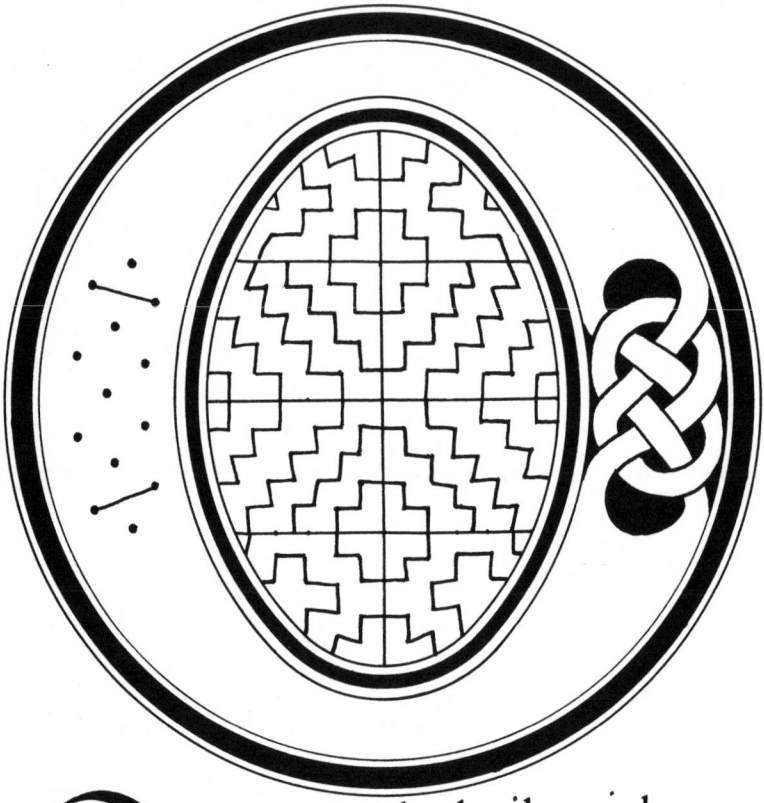

O, too, may be built with compasses, next page. Note the knot construction. The inner void is filled with steps.

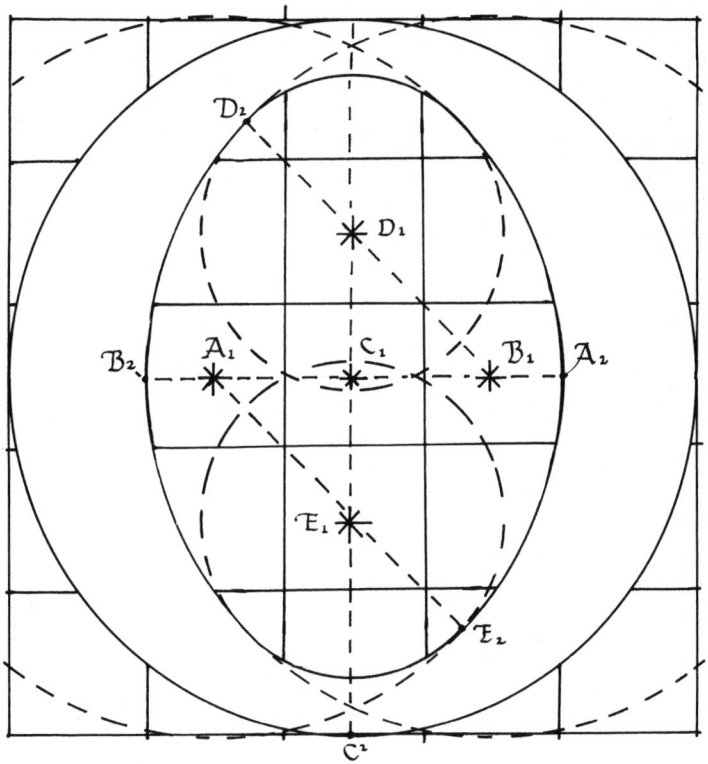
D2
D1
B2
A1
C1
B1
A2
E1
E2
C2

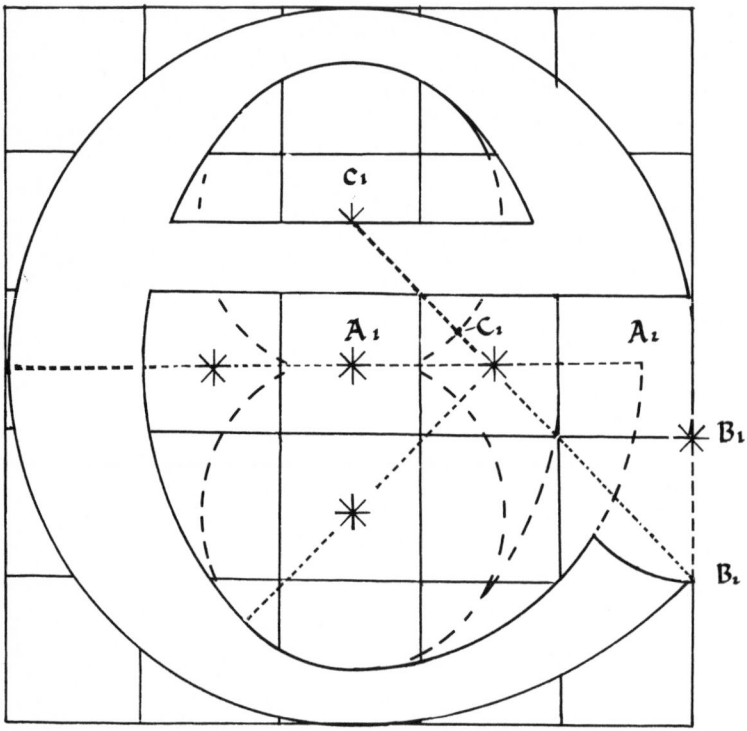


E follows the geometry of O, but for the curve of the tail; $A_1A_2$; $C_1B_2$. If not following the geometry, use squared paper to plot the

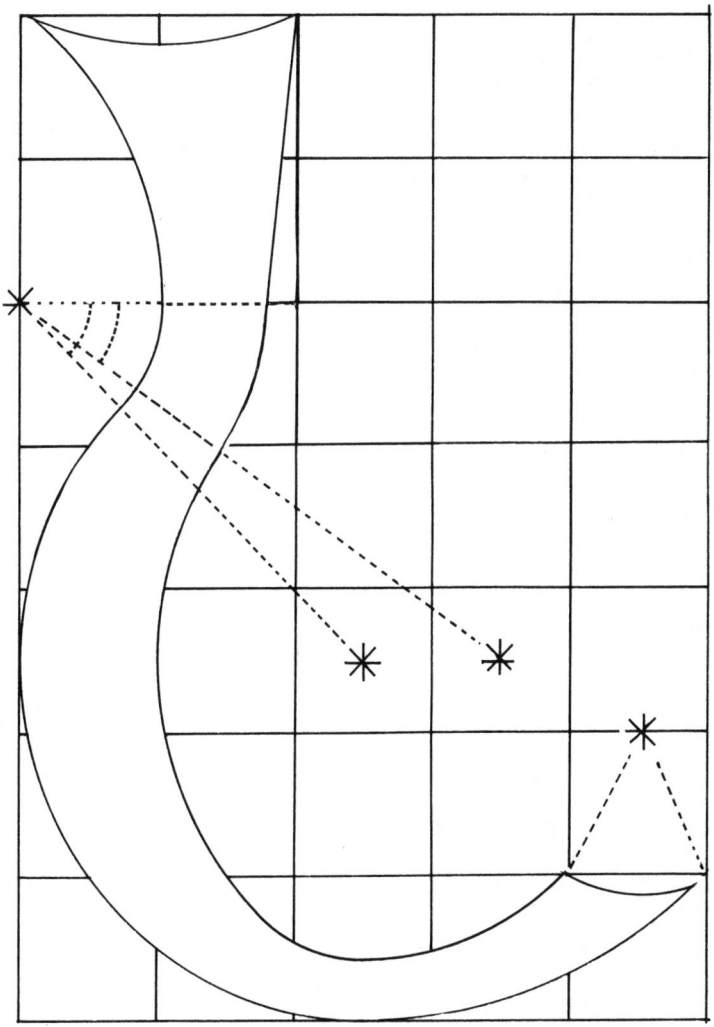

letters, trace and transfer.

The form of the majuscule L, overleaf follows from E, and introduces our grid for ascenders, b d h l, and descenders, f g j k p q x y z : 5 x 7. The descender of f, k, x, z is characteristic of the archaic script. Now f, k, are ascenders, while x, z have joined the mid-height tribe based on i: m, n, r, u, w; and on o: c, e, s, t, x.

It may also be remarked that here the letters are not capitals, to which we are accustomed; but although the old a, b, c, d, e, f, g, h, i, k look like small letters, or **minuscules** they originally had the status and dignity of formal capitals.

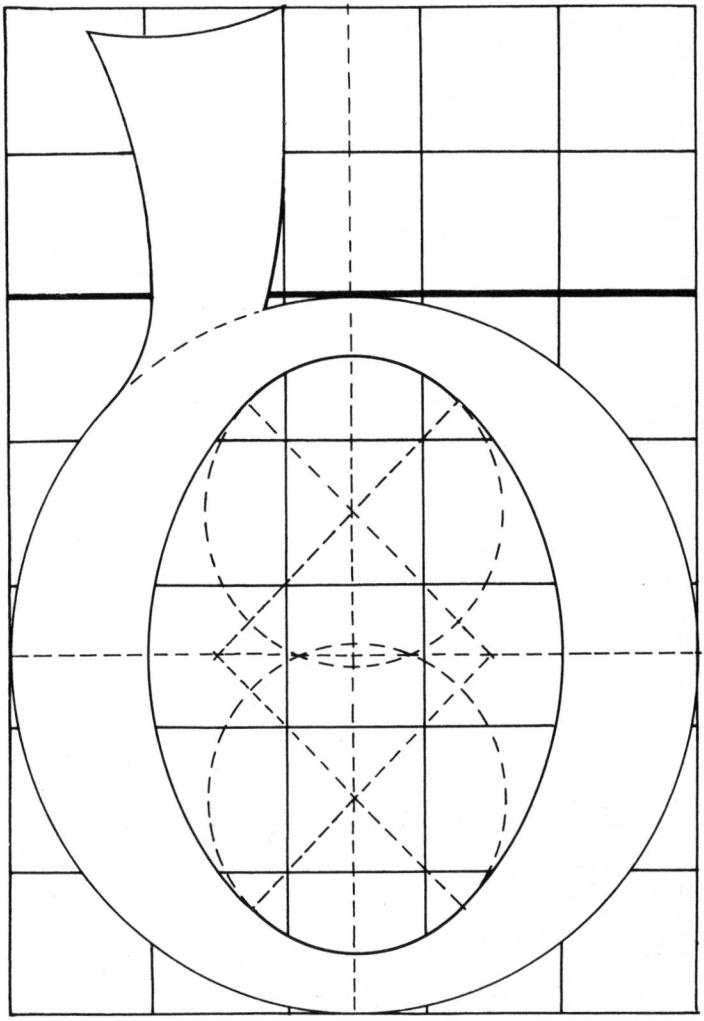

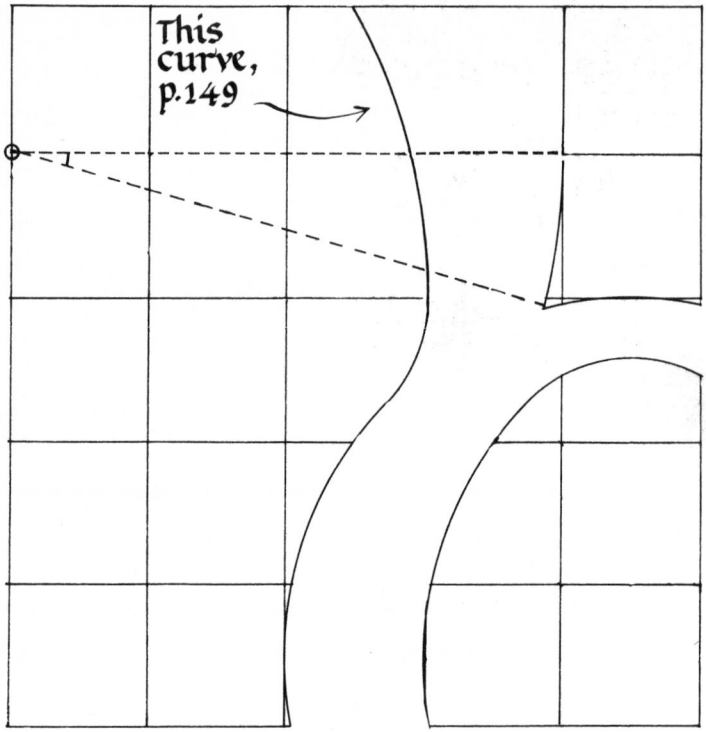


COMPARE the top of the B with that of L, p. 111. This narrower, blunter serif is preferable.

WHILE the body of B follows from O, the D stems from C. C has the same tail as E. H is likewise close to N, p. 106 & 118.

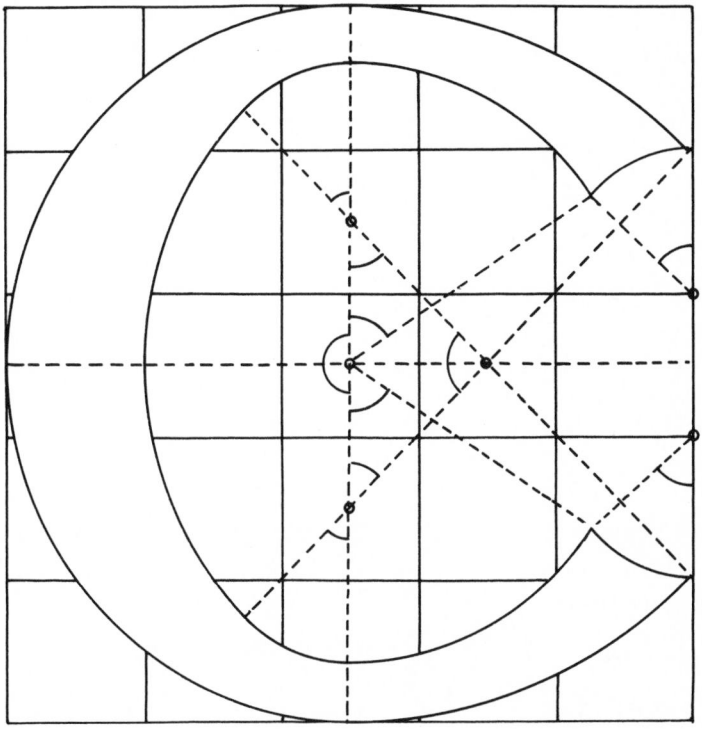

There are two curves to the serif of D.

This concludes the ascenders.

Next, 119-127, the descenders: F, G, J, K, P, Q, X, Y, Z.

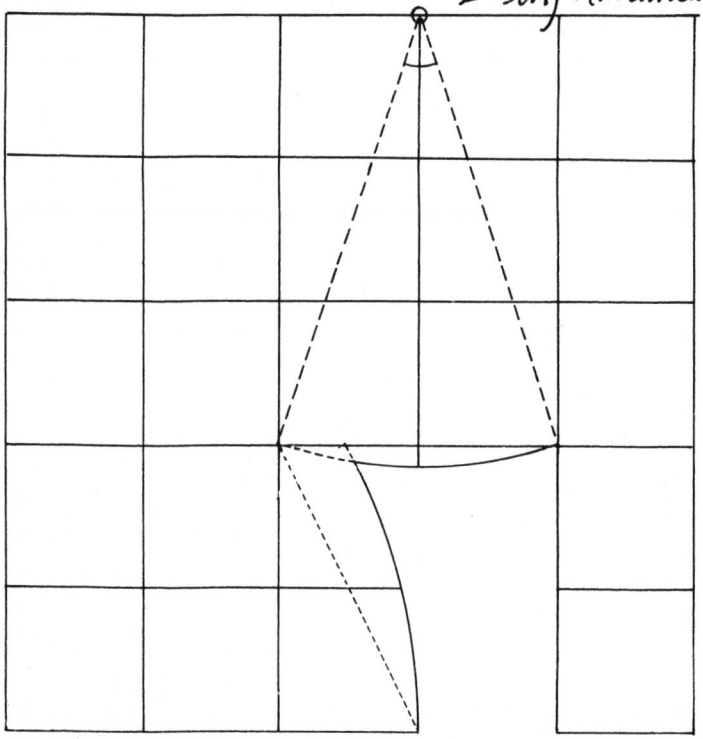

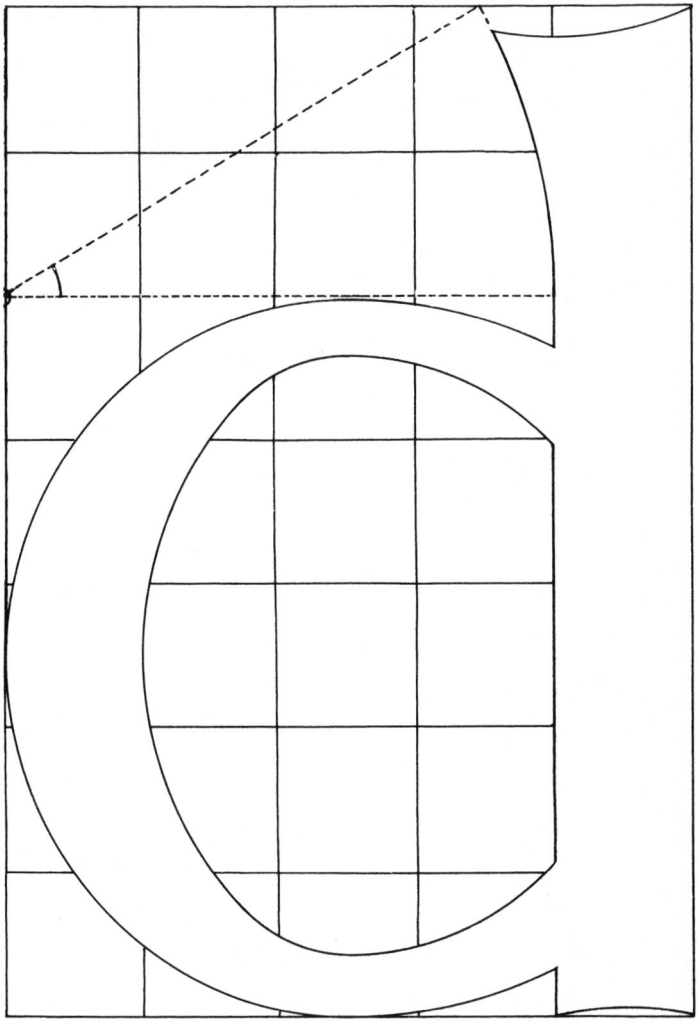

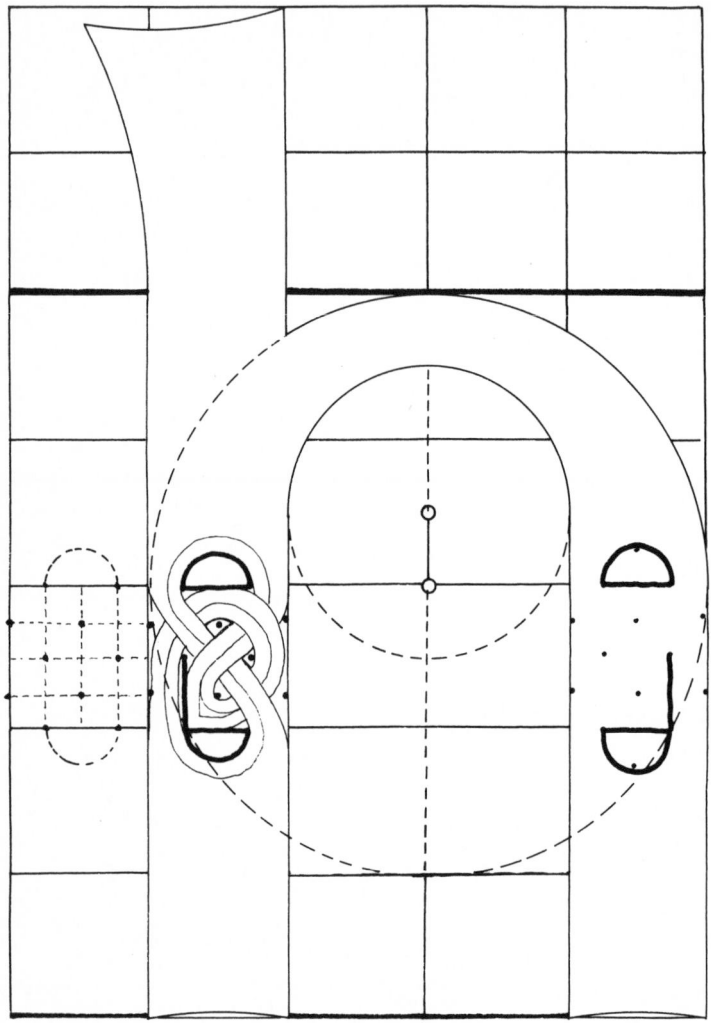

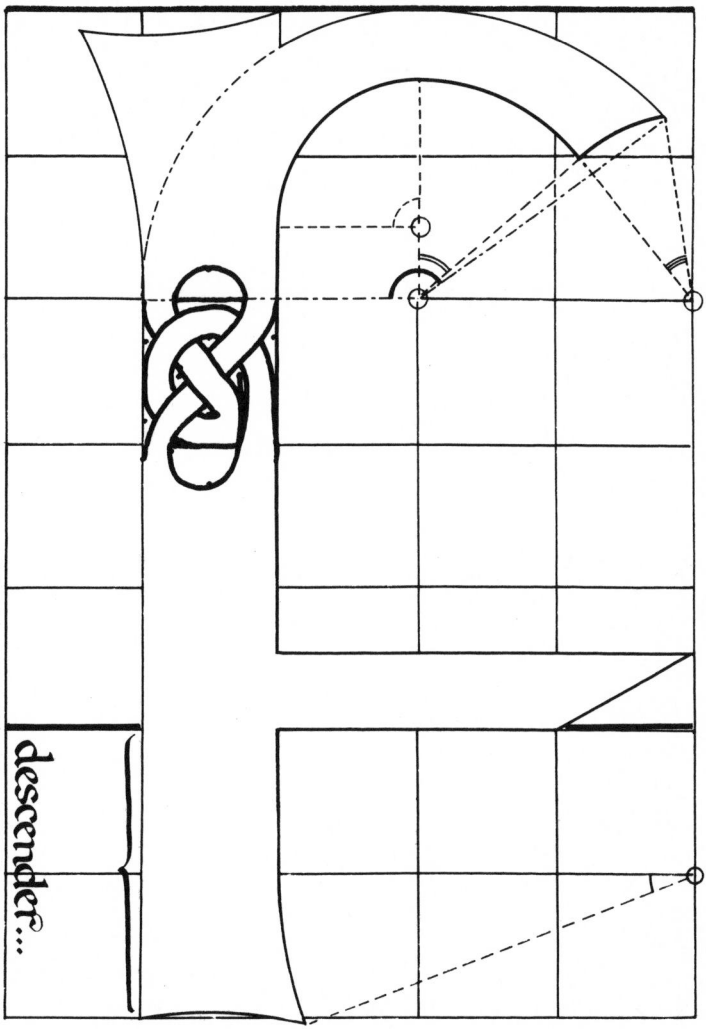
descender...

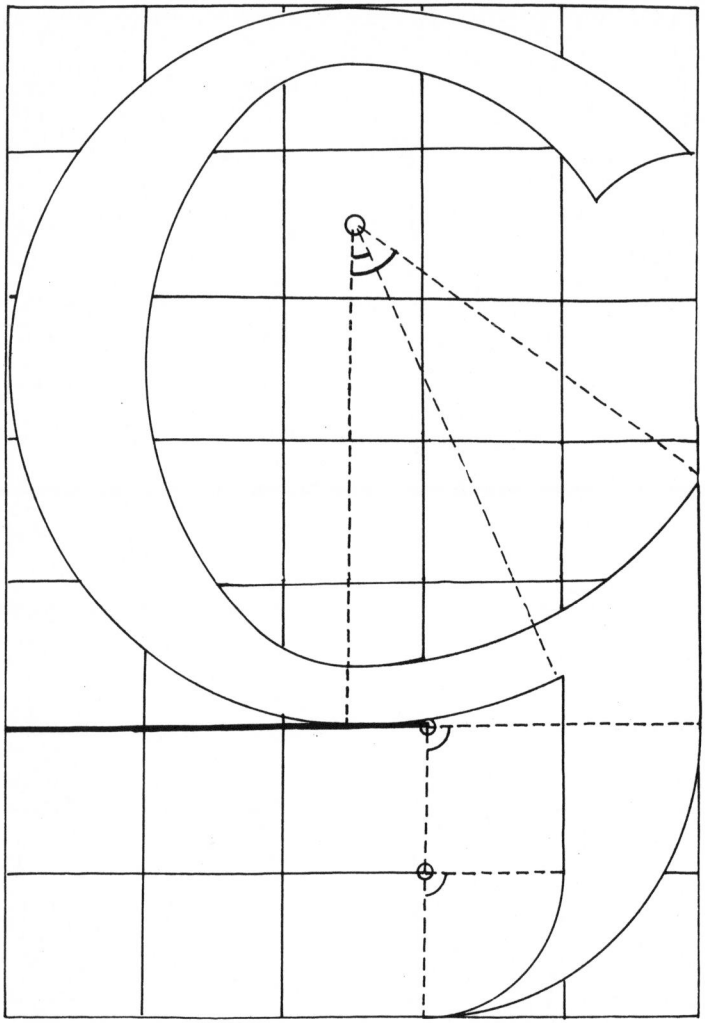

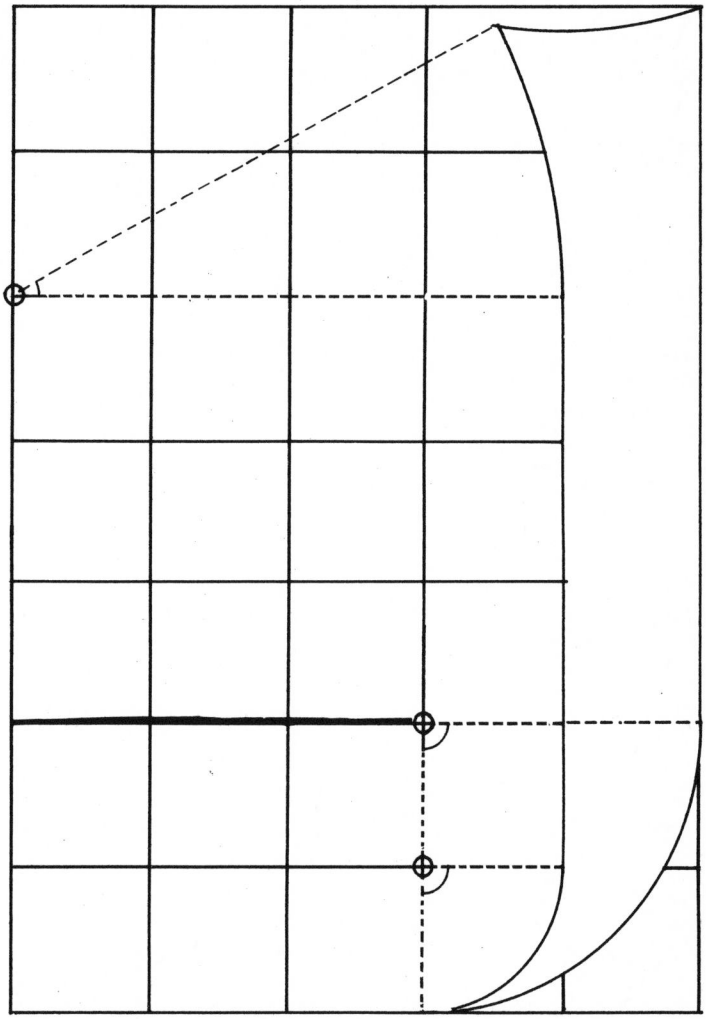

# Chapter VII

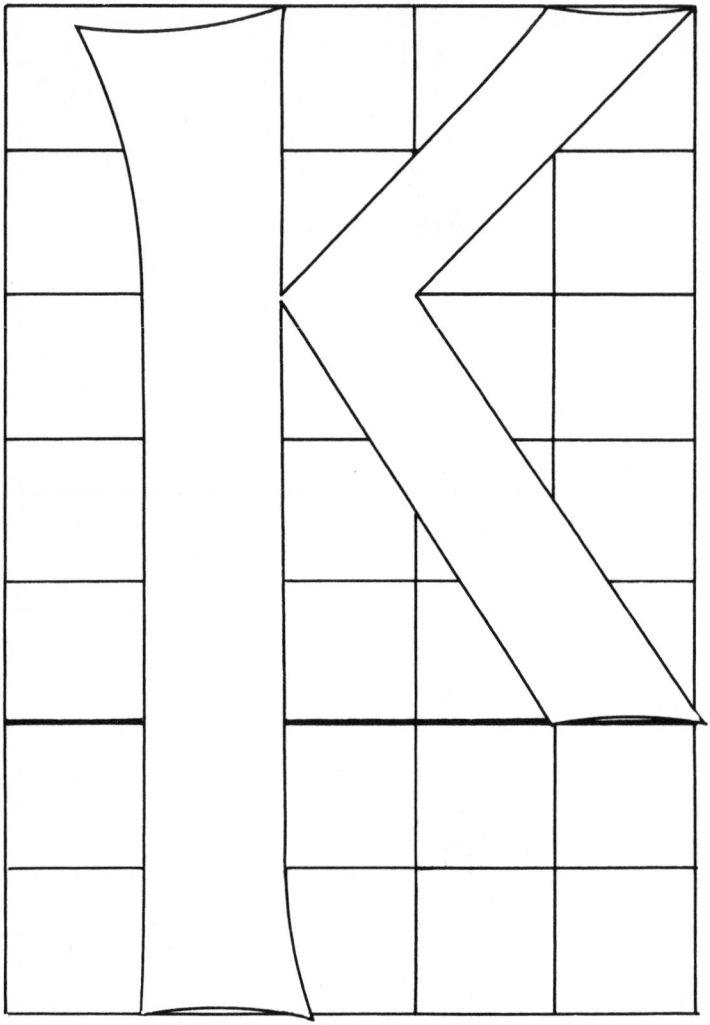

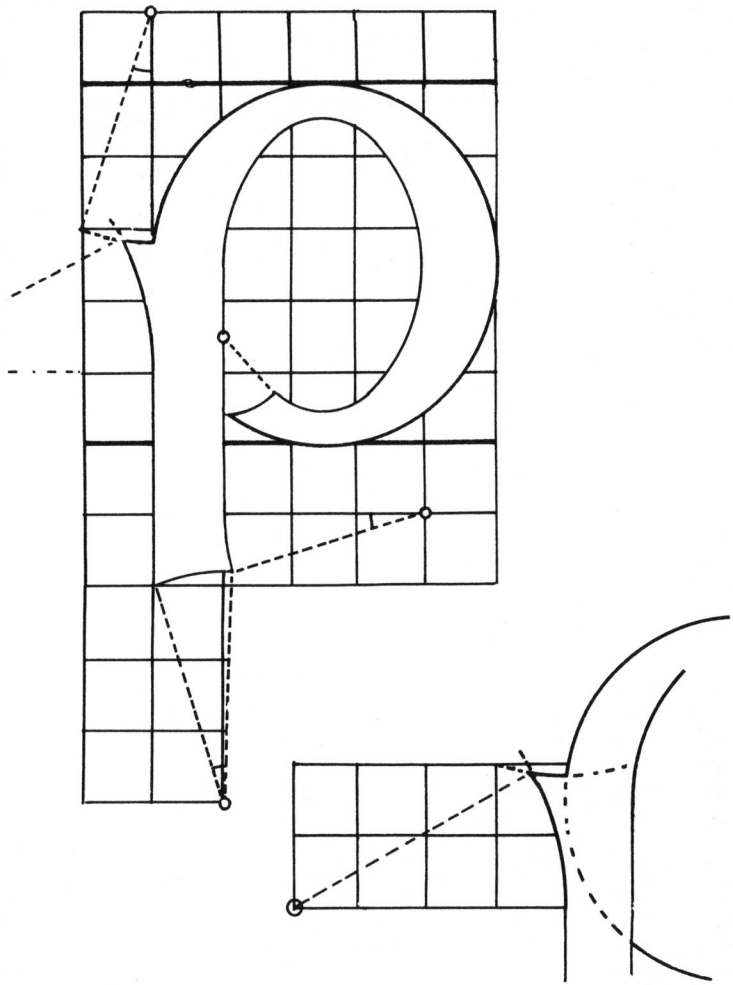

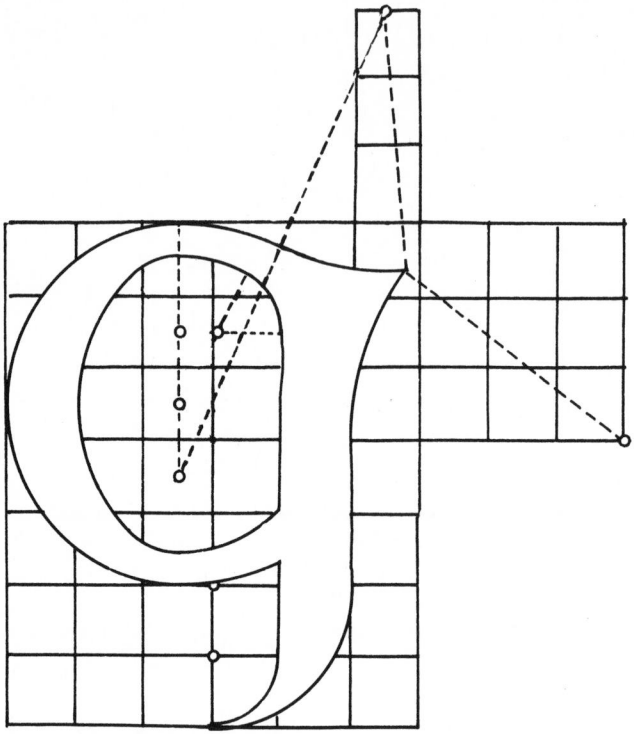

YES, this is Q, in the Celtic alphabet. It can be given a flat foot to match P, too.

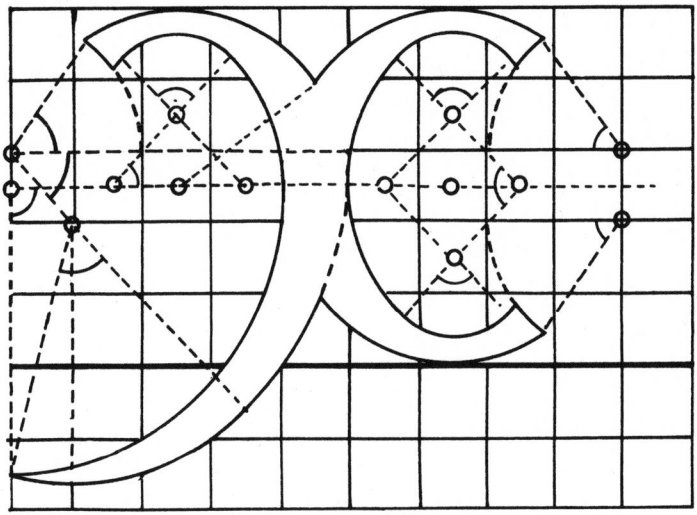

The X is a descender, as we see here. Each half is a cut-off O, with the tail added, sweeping away below leftwards. Or, equally, it could be done symmetrically; the left reflecting the right.

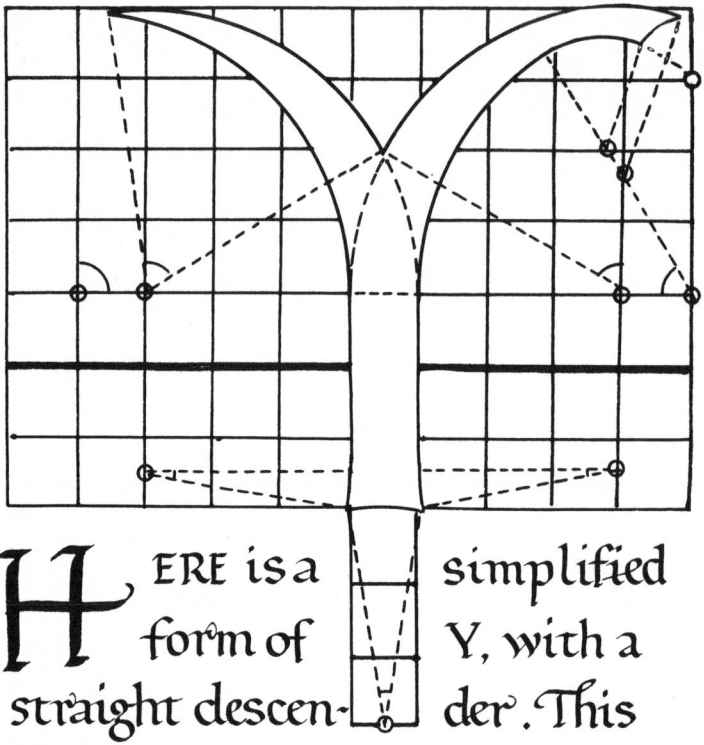

HERE is a simplified form of Y, with a straight descender. This foot is quite symmetrical. A curve, as in Q, would do as well. The sharp prong could be re—

peated on the right.. Y, like G, is pretty versatile. So is the celtic ZED: those dots are centres for drawing the succession of arcs

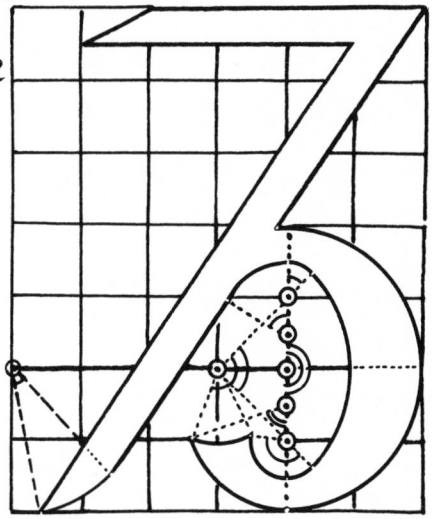

that may be compass drawn to produce the spiral tail.

WHICH brings up the point, WHY bother with the geometry at all?

# Chapter VII

As forms, letters are pen-made shapes. When a letter is to be decorated, however, it may be drawn freely or with compasses. Many including myself find it easier to draw a straight line with a ruler, a curve with compasses. So here is an alphabet of letters produced by compasses and ruler entirely. By this means, sharp, controlled, well-proportioned and lively shapes may be obtained. Few can do this free hand on a large scale, so here the letters are given along with their geometry. Besides, it really is fun to do, and compass work is an essential element of early Celtic art. This is good practice.

As well as ascenders and descenders there are the letters with neither, namely:

aceim

orstu

vwnd*

* this letter has two forms, an ascender, d, and the flattened form, ɒ, as here.

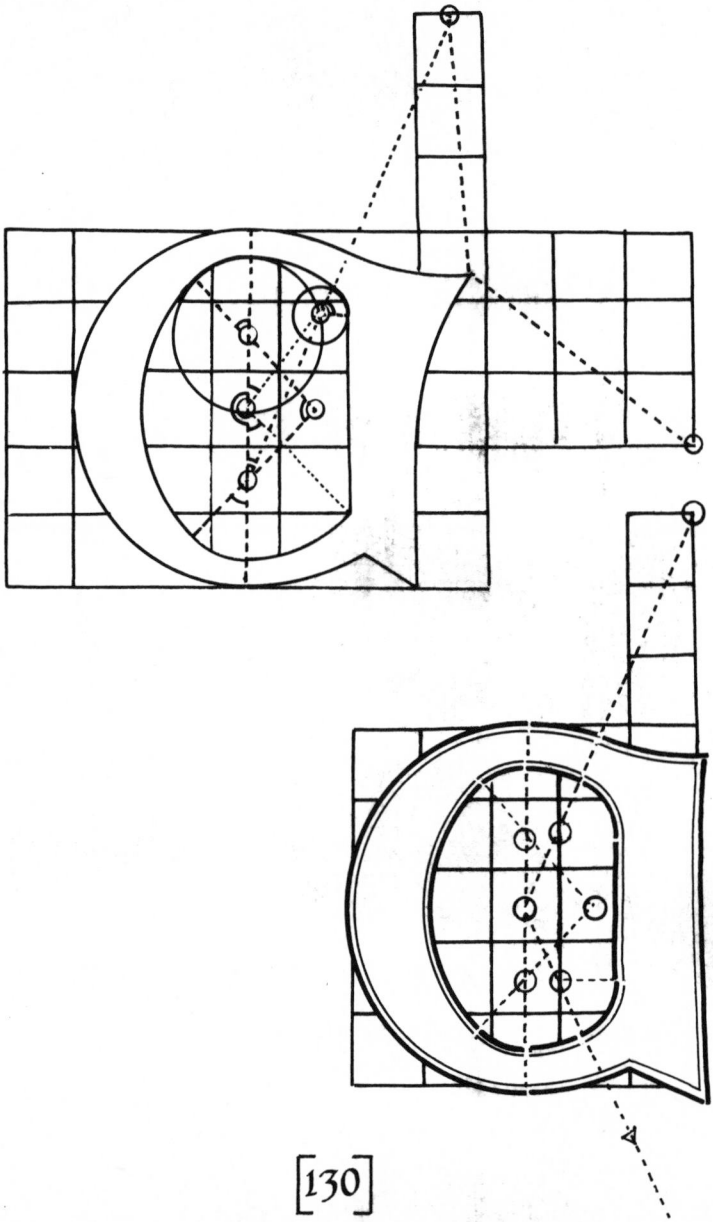

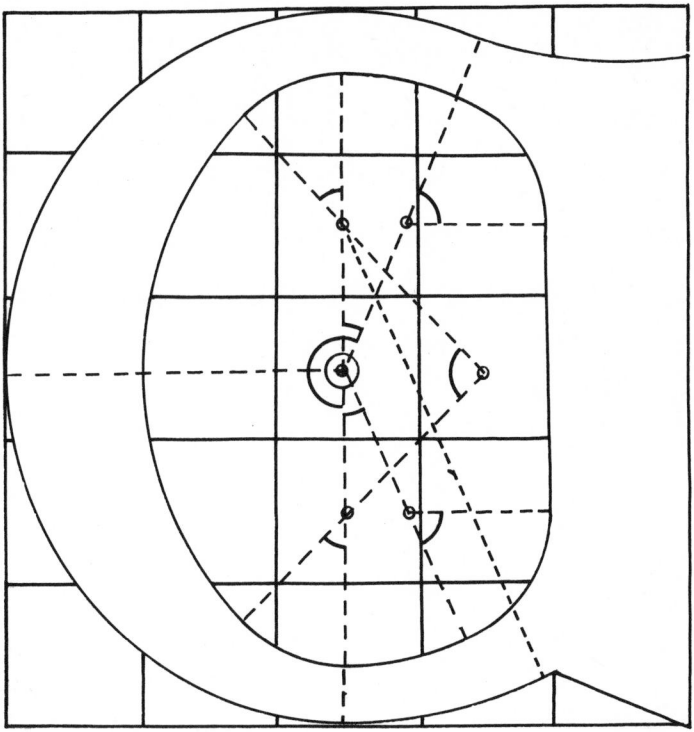

This page, as below, opposite, a simple form of the Celtic letter, a. Opposite, above, a variation of the serif, like that of a, on page 124.

INSTEAD of decorating the letter with a plain knot, it can be done with animal-shaped, zoomorphic pattern based on a knot, as here. Each snake has two long ears, laced into the weaving body-ribbons.

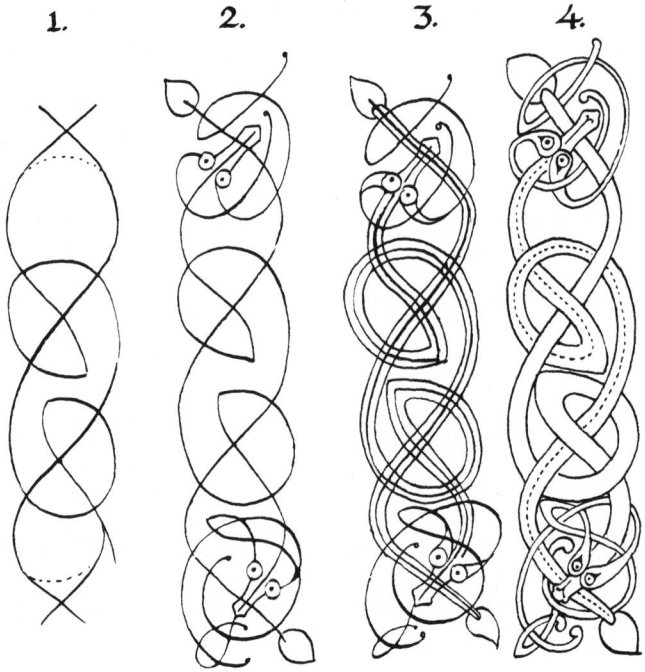

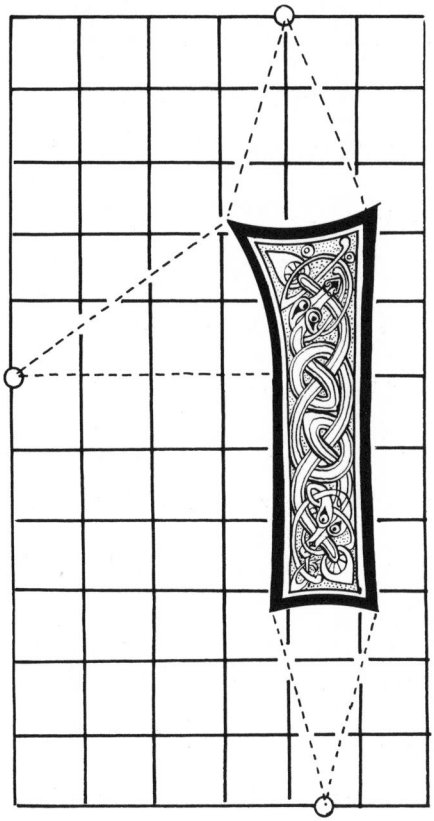

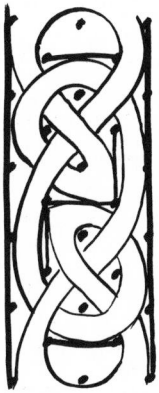

construction of the knot used here in the snakes.

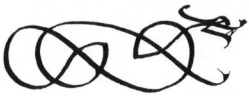

R: The stem of this letter is made the same way as 'l'. The curve uses five centres, 3 for the outside, top left, opposite page. HERE'S HOW: draw the arc 1, with the compasses fixed at centre 1. With the same centre, repeat the curve of the outline; step the fixed point to centre 2 and draw arc 2, inline and outline; continue arc 3 with centre 3.

FOR the inside curve, keep the centre at 3, and draw inside curve 3, see figure lower right. Continue the inline (thin) and outline (thick) through curve and centre 4: ditto from centre 5.

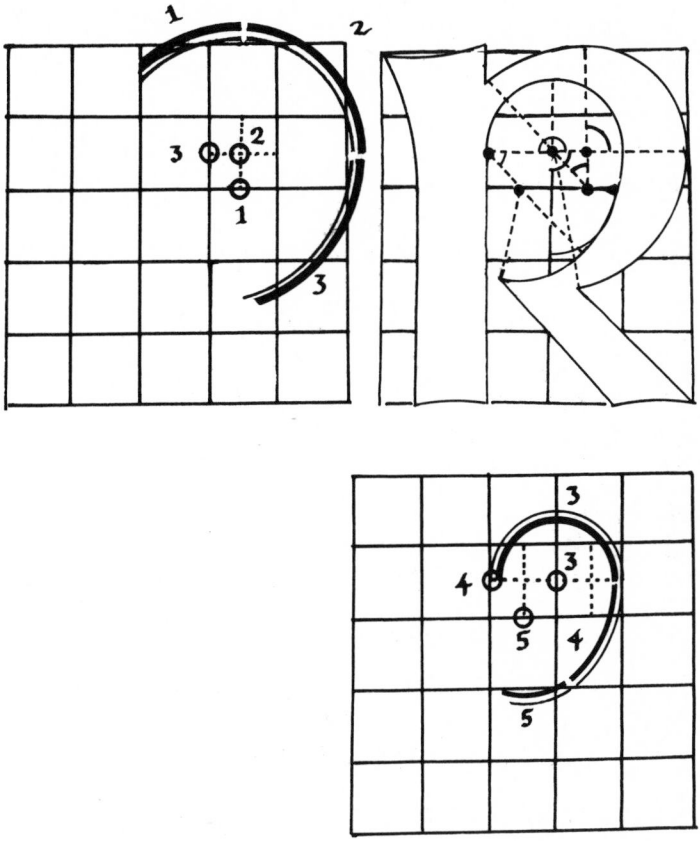
1
2
3
2
1
3
3
3
4
5
4
5

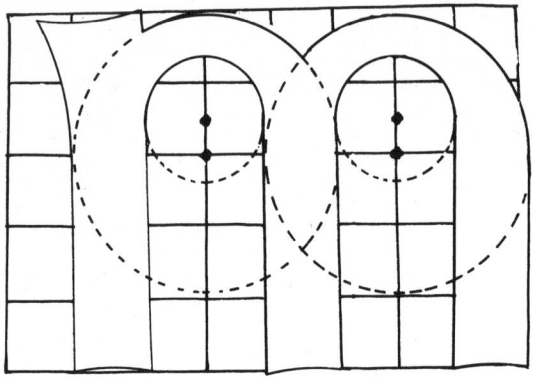

**m:** the steps for drawing 'm' are as follows:
lightly pencil a grid, 8 x 5.
Draw the stem, as for 'l'.
Pencil the circles, straight rule the legs.
Extend the grid to draw the hollows on the head & feet serifs,

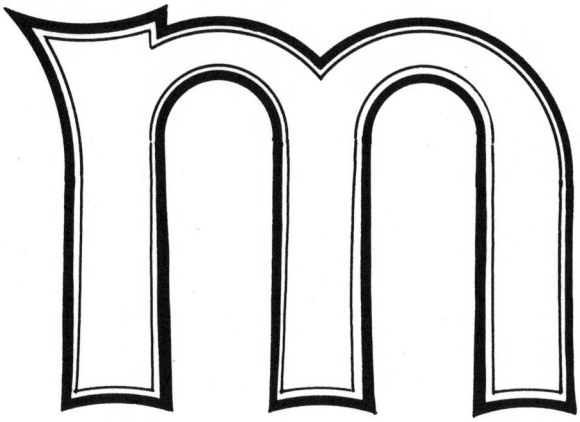

as shown on page 133.
In drawing the letter, start at a point, say upper left, then draw each curved line or straight line section continuously, each new line starting precisely on and springing from the end of the last one; progress around the out-

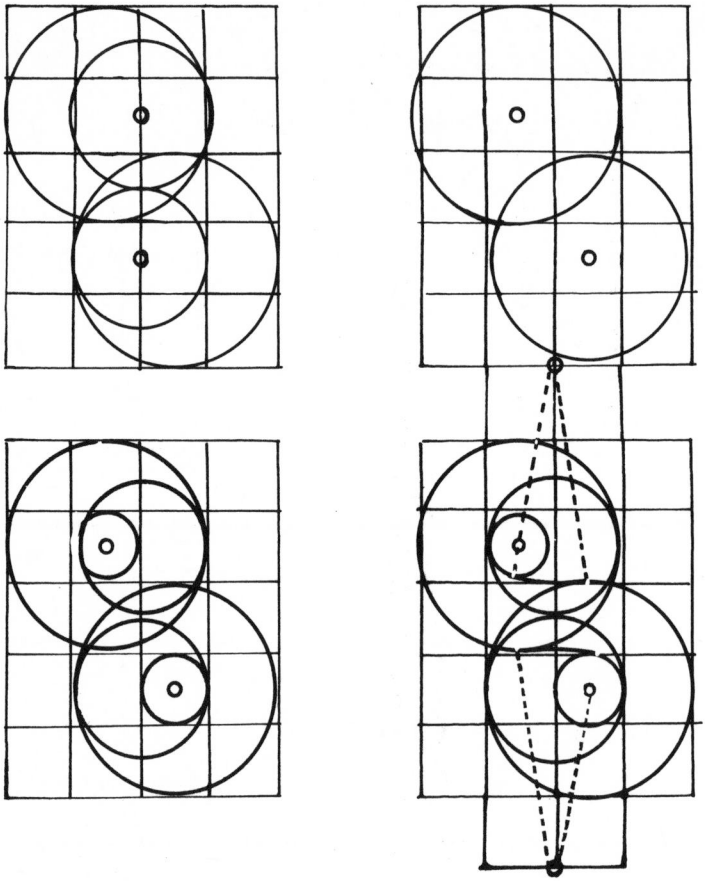

line, doing thin and thick lines together. Then repeat, in ink.

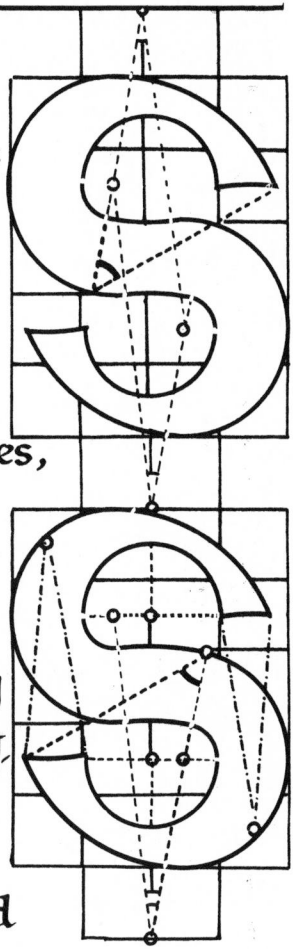

S first pencil the circles as on page 138, then the head and tail, here, above. The waist can be done from two centres, making it concave, or from one centre as here, below. All the centres may be found from points on the grid, or the crossing of lines between established centres.

T: the body of 'T' is like 'C' on page 115 above.

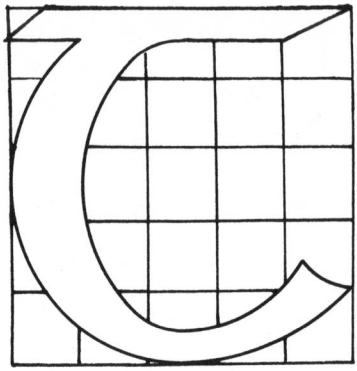

U: opposite: extend the square grid to make the head and foot serifs on letters such as 'U'. If you are inking up the letter close to the edge of the page and find you have not enough room, you can extend the page by slipping another sheet alongside and partly under the first, and taping it.

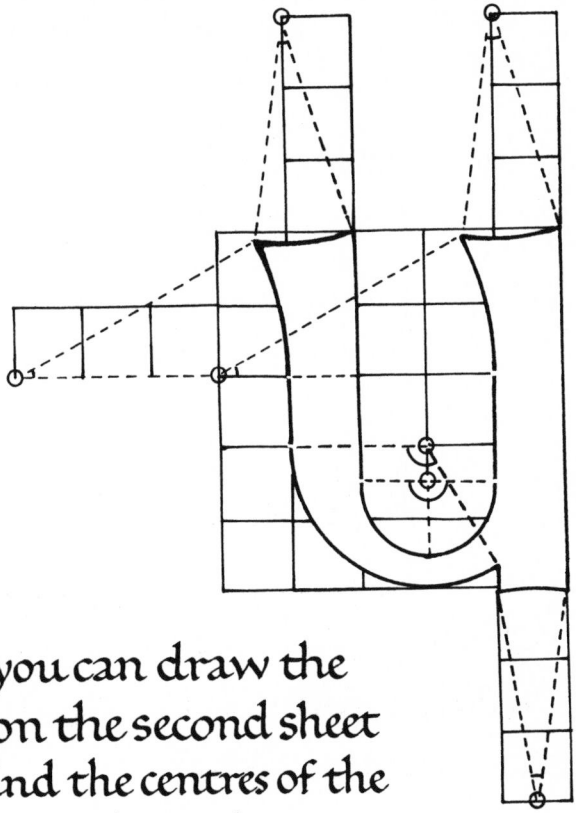

Then you can draw the grid on the second sheet and find the centres of the curves, as shown here.

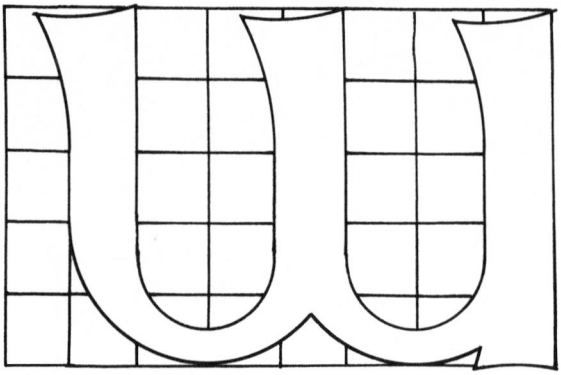

# W:

here the letter is made up of 'U', as on the previous page. Another form is the 'Double-Vee', as opposite, above.

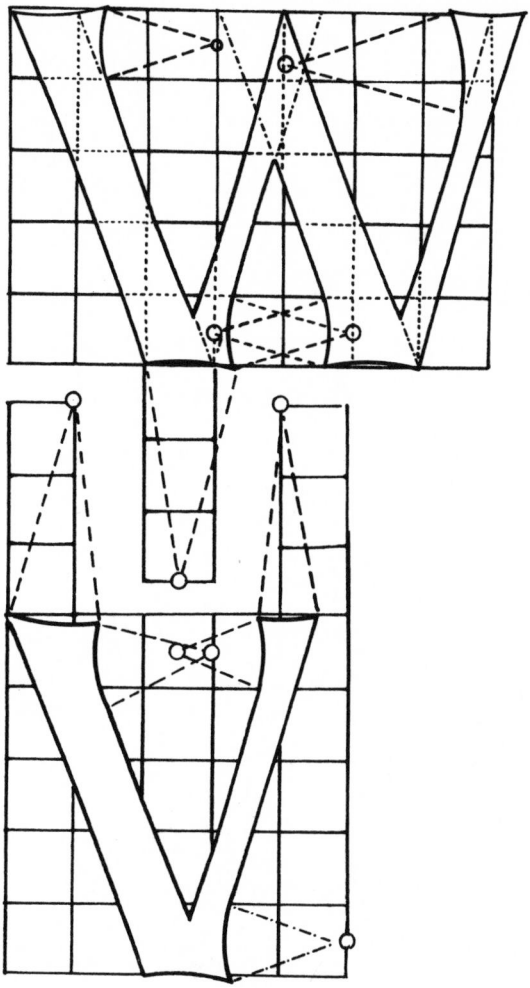

## Conclusion

The letters here may be decorated with step patterns or key patterns. Use the illuminated letters you make as initials, personalised monograms, greeting cards, gift labels, fabric paintings etc. The patterns may be used in themselves wherever ornamentation is called for in art or in decor, in textiles, tiles, metalwork, woodwork, murals; the applications are as many as may be imagined. With pen and paper you can easily master the patterns in this book. Then look around and apply them in your own life, however you may feel inspired. The aim of this book, and that of the entire series of "Celtic Design", will thereby be fulfilled: the revival of Celtic art.

HERE is how you can divide the side of a square into five equal parts; the same means may be used to divide any straight line into any number of parts:

- Rule a line AB at not too steep an angle to corner of square, at B; the line is longer than the side of the square.
- Set dividers to what you guess to be about 1/5 of the side of the square, and step off this measure, 1 ~ 5.
- Put SETSQUARE so it passes through corner of square & point 5, place ruler against setsquare; HOLD RULER STILL, and slide setsquare along to point 4.

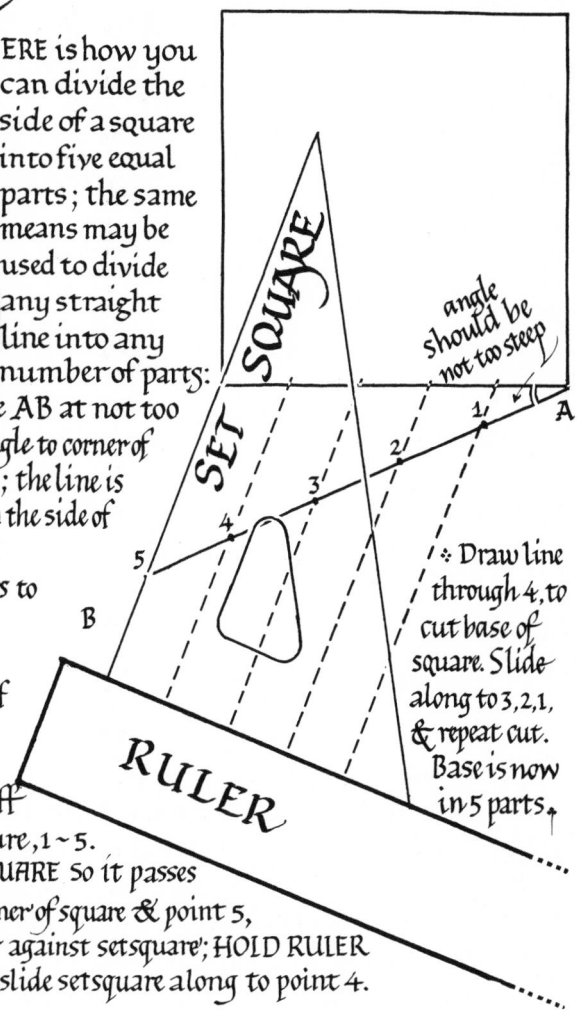


- Draw line through 4, to cut base of square. Slide along to 3, 2, 1, & repeat cut. Base is now in 5 parts.

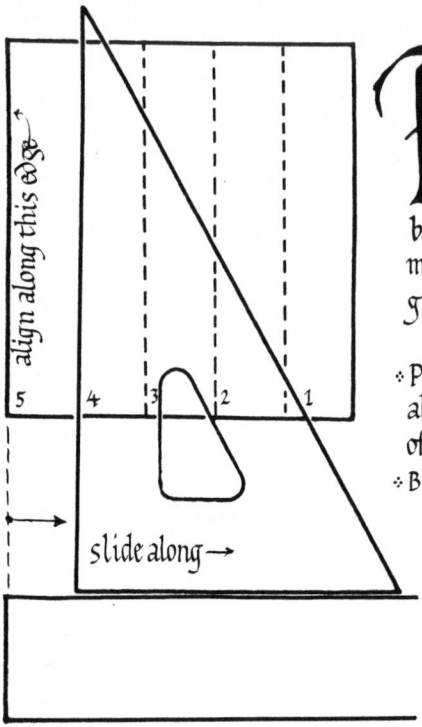


HAVING set off the five part division of the base of the square, the square may now be divided in a 5x5 grid, thus:

- Place the set square flush along the upright, left side of the square.
- Butt the ruler up against the horizontal edge of the set square.
- Slide the set square along the ruler, to point 4, and rule the vertical line to cut the top edge.
- Now slide along the ruler to point 3, and rule across the square to cut the upper edge.
- Carry on until the square is divided by lines cutting through points 2 and 1.
- N.B. throughout, keep ruler steady. If it moves, move the set square back to the edge and butt the ruler back into line.

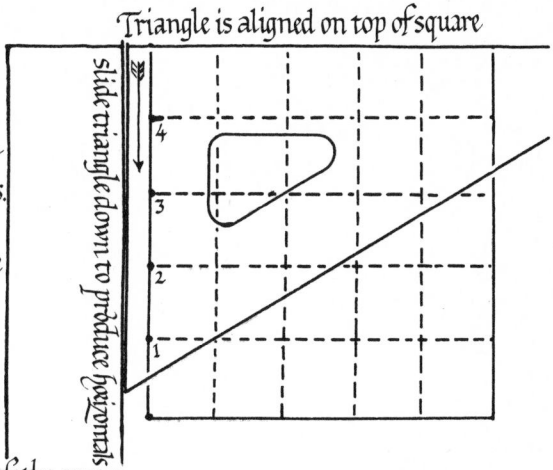


NOW for the horizontal lines.

- Open the legs of the dividers to the width of the 1/5 division already established along the base of the square. Walk this unit up the side of the square.
- Line up the set square along the top edge. The vertical side of the triangle is a little to the left of the square.
- Butt the ruler against the upright side of the square.
- Using the ruler as a guide track, slide the triangle down to point 4, and draw the horizontal across.
- Likewise, produce remaining latitudinal parallel lines at points 3, 2, 1, to complete the 5x5 grid.

The grid can be extended beyond the square with the ruler, by projecting the horizontal and vertical lines. To make a grid 8 across and 5 down, first extend the square by producing all the horizontal lines. Step off the 1/5 of the square to three spaces as before; place ruler horizontally below the figure as on previous page, as a rail along which to slide the set square and thus complete the grid.

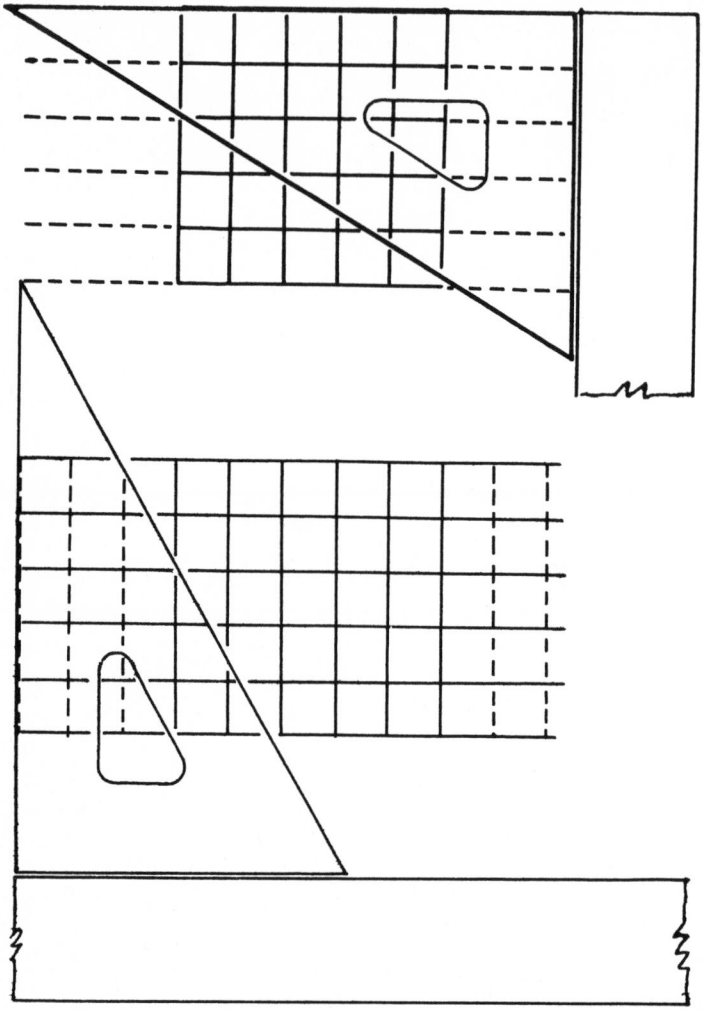

THE set square and ruler may be used to extend a grid on either side of the square, not only to lay out a wide letter, but also to find centres for serifs and such which may lie off the area to one side or the other. With a pair of dividers, a set square and a straight edge, a grid may be extended indefinitely, horizontally or vertically. As Celtic patterns are based normally on grids, it is necessary to know how to construct such a grid. The alphabet here presented provides an opportunity to develop skill with these tools of design.

USE the triangle to layout a page of text like this: with the top of the page as a horizontal, and the triangle flush with this, set the corner of the set square to the left of the left-hand margin and set the ruler against the vertical side of the triangle. Hold the ruler firmly between thumb and middle finger, slide the triangle down to the point on the margin line for the top of the text, and hold it there with the index finger of the left hand; the finger on the triangle need not press as heavily as the two on the ruler. With the right hand, draw the horizontal rule, while the left holds the ruler & triangle steady. Should the ruler slip, begin again. It may slip if you relax your pressure on the ruler, forgetfully. This initial tendency is remedied by practice. If the ruler swivels, however, it may be bowed, and should therefore be discarded and replaced. If you use wood rulers, get two at a time, to cover the possibility of warpage in one of them.

Having ruled the horizontal line marking the head of the text, next do the vertical margin lines: move the triangle to the corner of the text area, upper left, flush with the horizontal.

# Appendix

**A**: to establish the upper edge of the text block, place triangle along top of page; butt the ruler against the vertical edge of the triangle; hold the ruler in place with thumb and middle finger.

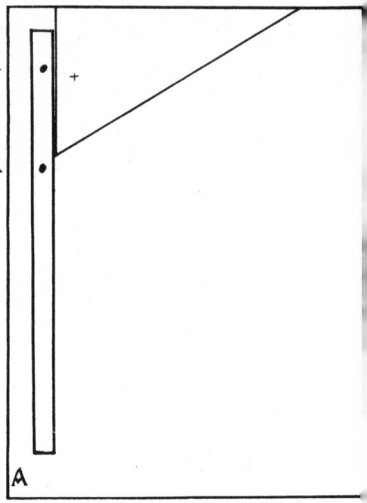


**B**: slide the triangle along the ruler to where you have decided the top of the text should be. Do this with one hand, keeping a firm pressure on the ruler all the while with thumb and finger. When the triangle is in position, hold it with the index finger of the hand holding the ruler. Thus one hand holds both ruler and set square, which leaves the other free to pencil the horizontal line atop the text block.

**C**: the horizontal line now becomes the guide for the left hand margin: slide the triangle over so that its corner coincides with that of the text block; butt the ruler against the set square; hold the ruler, take away the triangle, and rule the vertical.

**D**: likewise, the other side.

**E**: step the line spacing off on the left with the dividers.

**F**: mark the lower case "x-height" above the top line; with the dividers still at the line spacing as before, step off the spacing; with ruler and set square, rule.

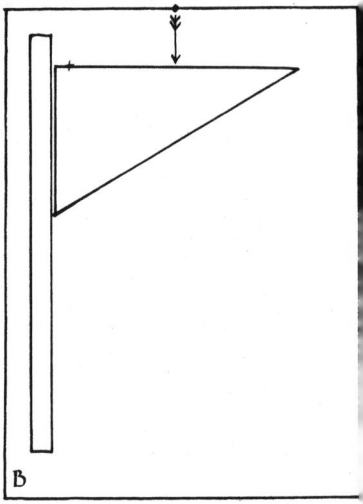

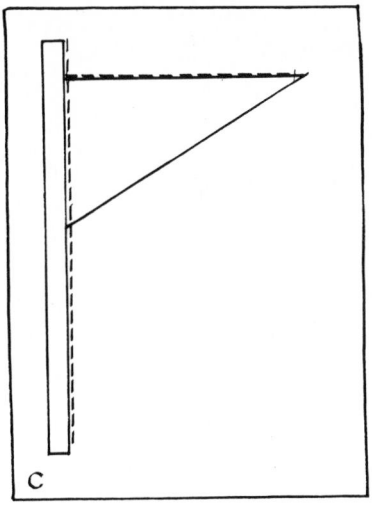
C

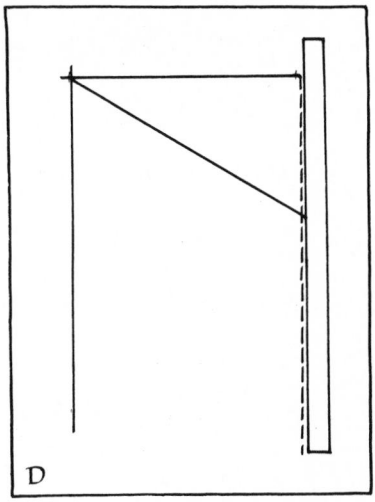
D

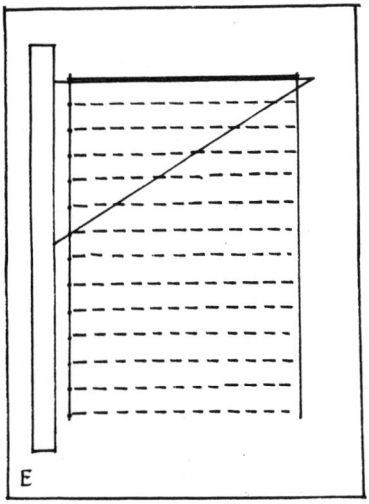
E

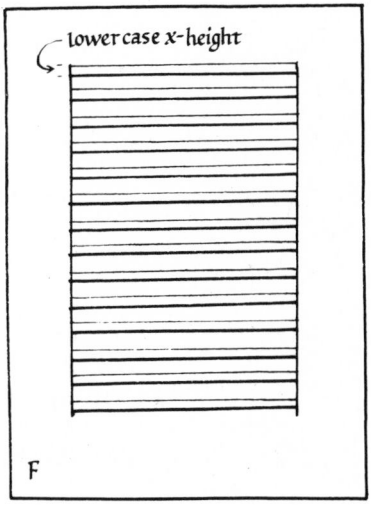
lowercase x-height
F

**Dividers:** this tool is used to divide a line into a number of equal spaces, as in ruling a page. In this case, the spacing is determined by *the width of the pen's nib.*

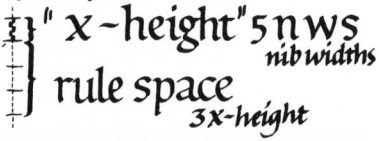


Five nib widths give the letter height of the letters *x*, o or *i*, called *x*-height; set off this unit on the top line of the text; set the dividers' legs 3 *x*-heights

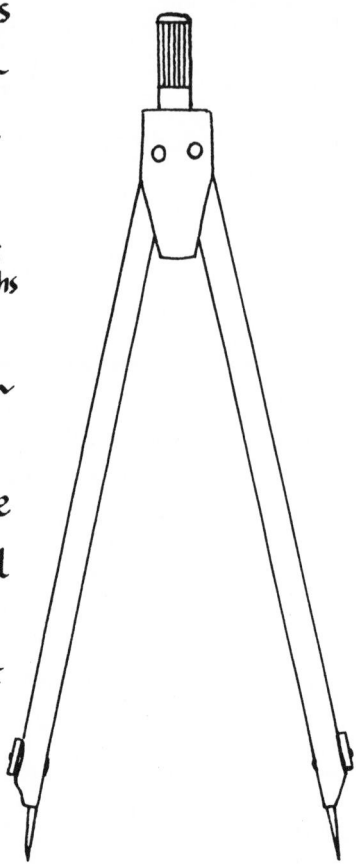

apart; set one leg at the point that is the intersection of the line already ruled as the top line of the text block and the left hand, vertical margin; step off the spacing down the vertical length of the text area, say 18 times, a standard number of lines to a page of script. Do not press too hard: pressure can alter the span of the dividers. These light pricks are to mark the base line rules; to measure off the top of the x-height above each of the rules, step off the dividers from the top of the x-height on the top row. *Provided the span of the dividers has not been altered at all*, the result will be a series of points, in pairs, pricked down the left margin. With ruler parallel to the margin, and set square, rule the page.

# Rulingpen:

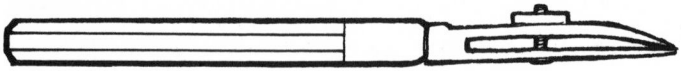

This, as the name implies, is a tool especially for ruling lines with ink. Ink may be applied with a dropper, or a brush. One drop is enough, and should be inserted between the blades of the nib. The screw controls the distance between the blade points, which determines line thickness: thinnest when closed, thicker when opened allowing a variety of effects. Provided the ink is contained within the blades, the pen nib may be drawn along the edge of a ruler, even a non-bevelled one, or a set square, with no smearing or running of ink.

Also, the ruling pen usually comes with a compasses in graphic art or drafting suppliers; the ruling pen nib is detachable from its handle, and can be interchanged with the pencil-lead attachment of the professional compasses. This makes it possible to draw perfect circles in ink, as in the geometrically drawn letters of the alphabet; by a combination of ruling pen for the straight lines, and compasses for the curves, the alphabet can be drawn entirely with tools, as we have seen, pp.102-143, above.

# Paper and Ink:

last but not least, for art and calligraphy good paper is necessary. You need some top grade paper, a few sheets of the best make available, for very special work. But for every day work you need a stock of paper which need not be hand made, sized, deckle edged or watermarked. You can get a single-ply Bristol Board, acid-free or 'P-H neutral', with a high rag content, which is quite serviceable and takes Chinese (*non waterproof*), Indian (*waterproof*) black inks; Tempera, Gouache, or designers' colours. Spirit-based inks may bleed on single-ply Bristol, though, and water colour wash cockles this paper.

The best ink is the stick sort, a little finger length of pressed carbon, bound in a medium of gum. This has to be hand ground in a slate slab, available at the supplier. A few drops, less than half a teaspoon, in the grinding stone is sufficient to dissolve the stick into a strong, solid black; too much water takes too long to blacken, as even a few drops may need ten minutes to rub to jet blackness. Alternatively, Chinese (or Japanese) sumi ë ink comes in bottles, ready to use. Indian ink is like Chinese ink, but with lacquer added to make it waterproof. Chinese ink is kinder to nibs and brushes, and washes out when dry, being non-waterproof.

# Appendix

While sumië ink is traditionally preferred by scribes, it is suitable for quill, or metal nib dip pens, but not for fountain pens. On the other hand, writing fluid for pens such as Osmiroid or Sheaffer, etc., which are commonly used by calligraphers, is generally either not light-fast, so the dye fades in sunlight, or is acidic, leaving an acid burn after the colour has faded; it also bleeds on paper where Chinese or Indian works fine.

Recently, a new fountain pen ink has been developed, *Pelikan Fount India drawing ink for Fountain Pens*.. it is opaque, light fast, and waterproof, and seems less gummy than plain Indian ink.